THE ESSENCE OF THE GARDEN

GARDEN DESIGN
AND STYLE

TRISHA DIXON

📚 Angus&Robertson
An imprint of HarperCollins*Publishers*

PHOTOGRAPHS APPEARING ON
PRELIMINARY PAGES:

TITLE PAGE: *Simple bush timber arches are softened with the prolific growth of old-fashioned climbing roses.*

CONTENTS, PAGE IV: *Elegant verandah steps under a mantle of autumn leaves.*

CONTENTS, PAGE V: *The classic but simple elegance of this pergola covered terrace provides a strong element of architecture in this country garden.*

AN ANGUS & ROBERTSON BOOK
An imprint of HarperCollinsPublishers

First published in Australia in 1991
Reprinted in 1992

CollinsAngus&Robertson Publishers Pty Limited (ACN 009 913 517)
A division of HarperCollinsPublishers (Australia) Pty Limited
25 Ryde Road, Pymble NSW 2073, Australia

HarperCollinsPublishers (New Zealand) Limited
31 View Road, Glenfield, Auckland 10, New Zealand

HarperCollinsPublishers Limited
77– 85 Fulham Palace Road, London W6 8JB, United Kingdom

Distributed in the United States of America by
HarperCollinsPublishers
10 East 53rd Street, New York NY 10022, USA

Copyright © Trisha Dixon 1991

National Library of Australia
Cataloguing-in-Publication data:

Dixon, Trisha, 1953 –
    The essence of the garden.

    Bibliography.

    Includes index.
    ISBN 0 207 16806 7.

    1. Gardens — Design. I. Title.

712

Front cover: Reflected sculpture. Kelton Plain, Cooma, NSW
Back cover: Pergola. Micalago Station, Michelago, NSW

Printed in Hong Kong

5 4 3 2
95 94 93 92

For Darvall, Skye and Hamish

CONTENTS

PREFACE

*And when your back stops aching
and your hands begin to harden
You will find yourself a partner
In the glory of the garden*

RUDYARD KIPLING, 1865–1936
'The Glory of the Garden'

I f, as Shelley once said, the first purpose of a garden is to give happiness and repose of mind, why is it that we *do* garden till our back aches and our hands begin to harden? Is it to express our artistic nature or to beautify our surroundings? As that great gardening writer, Vita-Sackville-West jotted in her *Country Notes*, the gardener is one of the fortunate people concerned wholly with beauty. 'Fortunate gardener, who may preoccupy himself solely with beauty . . . he is one of the few people left in this distressful world to carry on the tradition of elegance and charm . . . he must not be denied his rightful place. He deserves to share it, however humbly, with the painter and the poet.'

Fortunate gardener indeed, to be totally occupied with creating beauty, but to what ends. A garden should not be a status symbol. Neither should it be a millstone

A B O V E :   *The appropriate addition to any country courtyard — a gaggle of geese.*

O P P O S I T E :   *A canopy of greenery dapples the light onto the path below, creating a delicate sense of semi-enclosure. The simple but gracious lines of this pergola emanate from the generous proportions.*

around our necks. It should indeed be, as Shelley was surely alluding to, a haven or retreat. That great Australian designer, Edna Walling, wrote that the nicest garden owner she knew was the little lady who said 'I don't want to grow flowers, I want to grow scenery'. To beautify our surroundings is the gardener's intent. And what better medium to express our artistic inclination.

So, what is the essence of the garden? Is it in the plants, the design, the surroundings, the fragrance or a mystical combination? It is certain that every garden evokes a distinct response. While many may concur in plant tastes or in matters of design, there are no two gardens the same. This, I feel, is the essence — individuality. How immensely pleasing that each garden is unique. What pleasure for each creator to cast his or her own spell.

Gardening is about inspiration — creating garden pictures, designing, and selecting plants. It is a blending of our creative, practical and physical skills. Whereas some gardeners are, by nature, plantsmen through and through, others look at a garden more in terms of design, that is, architecturally, in which case the plants are purely a means of implementing or softening the scheme. But how to be disciplined, if indeed we must. If, as Kay Overell wrote in the *Australian Garden Journal* 'your best, most looked-upon beds usually end up looking like a dog's dinner because you get greedy and want everything you love in them' perhaps the wonderful abundance of the cottage garden is more your garden style. However, even Gertrude Jekyll, that great exponent of the cottage garden style wrote: 'I am strongly of the opinion that the possession of a quantity of plants, however good the plants may be themselves and however ample their number, does not make a garden; it only makes a collection'. She goes on further to say that 'given the same space of ground and the same material, they may either be fashioned into a dream of

beauty . . . or they may be so misused that everything is jarring and displeasing. To learn how to perceive the difference and how to do right is to apprehend gardening as a fine art'. How much easier to write or talk about than accomplish. Far easier for a designer to be disciplined when drawing up plans than the gardener with a genuine love of plants.

The very soul of the garden lies in that fragile equilibrium between design and planting; regimentation and chaos. While the 'bones' or framework of the garden is perhaps the most important element, embellishment and artistry complete the picture. Once the garden structure is finalised, it is the gardener, by dabbling in colour, plant combinations, texture, space and general orderliness, who weaves a web of poetic artistry from which the garden truly evolves. While creative adroitness is very much the essence, so unfortunately are the more 'ho-hum' aspects such as time and funds.

I empathise with Anne Scott-James (*Down to Earth*) who made her garden with 'too little time, money and professional help, full of imperfections but a continual source of pleasure'. The real gardener, she writes, has weeds, failures, dirty fingernails and chapped hands, but enjoys the making and working. 'This is the way most people garden, always pushed hard for time and cash, the reality never quite catching up with the dreams. Most of us are quite content with the lack of perfection' she writes, 'for there is more pleasure in making a garden than in contemplating a paradise'.

Paradise or not, gardens take years to evolve. While some people are born with an innate sense of design or style, there is still much to be mastered in the pursuit of horticulture. Knowledge comes from simple trial and error — in plant selection, placement, nourishment and custody. Paths need to be planned and constructed, service areas thought about, fences or screens agonised over, and plans and schemes fantasised. Just as writers must study both the classics and modern literature, and sheepbreeders study genetics and wool types, so gardeners enjoy contemplating, analysing and scrutinising their own and others' gardens; perusing, reflecting on, or studying garden literature; examining plant manuals; and talking to other gardeners. In gardening exists the capacity to create as simple or intricate a masterpiece as we have the ability to master. Whether we draw on other civilisations or ages for inspiration or break new ground; whether we simply put in a few punnets of annuals or create totally new garden areas each year; whether we have a passion for bold contrasting colours or prefer single theme gardens, this is totally our own choice. I deplore garden snobbery. We must be allowed to be individuals and not try to cast all in the same mould.

However, in looking for garden inspiration, we often have to look beyond our own realms. When we have studied our 'how to' books and plant references, there is still a need for visual inspiration. South of the equator, we have realms of encyclopaedic reference books on native flora and just as many on garden construction, but for stimulation, we often look to the wealth of enticing publications from European, British and American publishers. For this reason, *The Essence of the Garden* is intended as a photographic source book on international garden styles, features and seasons, with the emphasis on structural ideas for the garden rather than actual planting. It is not the aim of this book to take the place of a planting guide, so vast is the range of climatic and planting limitations. However, if this book helps provide inspiration for the humblest garden scheme, it has served its purpose.

TRISHA DIXON
May, 1991

FOLLOWING PAGES: *Garden style is immensely individual and to a large degree reflects the personality of the garden owner. Here, roses create a sense of romantic intrigue.*

GARDEN
STYLES

The CLASSICAL GARDEN

*To make
a garden, one must have a
great idea or
a great opportunity.*

SIR GEORGE SITWELL, 1860–1943
On the Making of Gardens

A strong element of architecture is the key to the classical garden. Vistas, lines of axis, sculpture, walls, paths, pergolas and hedges create an order within the garden, lending a sense of mastery over the environment. Such gardens provide year-round interest with the garden framework providing the 'bones'. Classic clipped hedging, strong symmetrical lines and a masterful use of stonework impart a pleasing sense of order.

Evergreen plants form the basis of the classical garden. Planting schemes are rigid and exacting using repetition to striking effect. The ephemeral flowers of the cottage garden have little use in the formal garden, except within the confines of a structured parterre edged with an evergreen hedge such as the dwarf box (*Buxus sempervirens*

A B O V E : *These stately cool white madonna lilies* (Lilium candidum) *lend an air of elegance to the classical garden.*

L E F T : *A mass underplanting of pink forget-me-nots enhance the classic beauty of tulips and provide a magnificent spring display.*

LEFT: *Simplicity in planting is a feature of the classical garden — evergreens provide the backbone of the garden whilst colour is provided by a select palette of plants rather than a mass of different varieties competing for attention. In this case, a burst of golden daffodils herald the awakening of spring.*

'Suffruticosa'), faster growing *Lonicera nitida* or *Westringia fruticosa*. Flowers are not a feature in this style of garden. A restrained use of colour and variety is more apt and the flowering plants that are utilised are either noticeable in their simplicity, such as the white flowering periwinkle (*Vinca minor*) for year-round greenery, or refined such as the more sophisticated forms of tulips or hyacinths. Tall evergreen hedges (yew, cypress,

Escallonia or *Pyracantha*) provide a solid backbone and a foil for any colour within or can be used as living walls.

Statuary is used to stunning effect, providing a focal point within the garden. The use of carefully selected statuary is another reason for keeping the planting scheme simple with a predominance of green, so as not to distract the eye from centre stage. Aged terracotta pots are just as

ABOVE: *The graceful form of this magnificent urn is accentuated by the soft underplanting of forget-me-nots.*

LEFT: *Dovecotes add a touch of whimsy to the classical garden.*

distinctive as costly antiques given the right setting and specimen. Special panache often comes from using a very ordinary plant such as French lavender, *Erigeron* or the white violet in a pot in a special location. While a single urn or pot can lend an exotic or dramatic air to an area of garden, a pair of pots can dress up a front entrance, gateway, seat or steps. Clipped bays have perennial charm, while a few tulips in a simple terra-cotta pot flowering gaily at the front door or entrance also have great appeal.

Long grass walks can have more impact than the usual formed path, giving an added dimension of lushness to the garden. While a strong line of symmetry is needed within the formal garden, curved lines can be used, if replicated. Garden edging can be just as effective arching around beds as in geometric precision.

O P P O S I T E : *The statue at the end of this path draws the eye and compels exploration.*

A B O V E :   *Design is paramount in the classical garden — lines of axis, vistas, sculpture and evergreen hedges create a pleasing order within the garden. This sense of architecture provides the bones of the garden and gives year-round appeal, appeal which is heightened from season to season by something as dramatic as the burst of spring colour in the form of these daffodils.*

In the strictly formal garden, whatever is put on one side of the main axis is duplicated on the other side. Vistas draw the eye through arches, gates, changes of level or along paths, to a distant object, be it seat, urn, statuary or gate.

The true test of a successful formal garden is its appeal midwinter. The stripped-back winter look reveals all, and while a gentle blanket of snow or even a thick coat of frost accentuates the symmetrical arrangement of the garden, it also hides much. Without the distraction of lush summer flowers or rich autumn hues, the framework is all important. The use of space is just as significant as the plant material and architecture.

The COTTAGE GARDEN

*God gave all men all earth to love
But since our hearts are small,
ordained for each one spot should prove
Beloved over all.*

RUDYARD KIPLING, 1865–1936

Cottage gardens symbolise all that is romantic and uncomplicated about gardening. Of all styles of gardening, it is the cottage garden that is the most relaxed and unpretentious. Scented ramblers spilling over doorways, winding pathways and a profusion of colour give an air of enchantment to the cottage garden.

Depending for its charm on simplicity, there is nothing contrived in this simple style. Mildly overgrown or disorderly plants simply add to the spell. This is not a garden for the fastidious — planting is haphazard, with bits and pieces collected from friends and travels popped in at random. While there is the occasional exotica, it is the

ABOVE: *White opium poppies* (Papaver somniferum) *add charm to the cottage garden when scattered throughout the beds.*

LEFT: *The blues and mauves of the larkspurs and the jacaranda tree blend beautifully with the creams, greys and soft greens in this historic garden.*

tried and true hardy perennials that form the substance of the cottage garden.

Cottage gardeners simply 'enjoy' their gardens. They are not slaves to them, and although they may spend days pottering around their flower beds, they do not aim for fussy correctness. Flowers are encouraged to naturalise, self-seeding in unlikely spots without thought of colour co-ordination or height. In a sense, these gardens thrive on neglect. Much of their attraction is their bountiful informality.

For many, the whole charm of a cottage style garden is its lack of obligation — the wilder the better. There is no pretence to clipped edges or studied planting design: rather, it is a veritable patchwork of colour with inviting pathways lead-

OPPOSITE: *The appeal of the cottage garden is its uncontrived beauty — natural mediums such as wood are chosen for fencing and seating and a cheerful mix of plants, including productive fruit trees, vegetables and herbs are grown in picturesque harmony.*

ABOVE: *The quintessential cottage home and garden — the main feature being the front path which is bordered by cottage favourites such as fragrant lavenders, roses, alyssum and love-in-a-mist.*

ing to secret corners or hideaway seats. With little restraint needed in choosing plant material, there is a simple delight in acquiring all types of plant material: plants and cuttings are freely given and taken.

Fragrance is very much part of the essence of the cottage garden and this comes from the abundance of old-fashioned roses, honey-suckle, lilacs and bulbs, intermingled with a profusion of herbs. Herbaceous perennials form the basis of the cottage garden — foxgloves, holly-hocks, paeonies, daisies, lupins, campanulas, stocks, delphiniums and irises. And what would a cottage garden be without roses, tumbling over fences and sheds and spilling onto paths, their poignant scent giving much to the charm of the

RIGHT: *The cottage garden is a place of uncontrived beauty, a gathering of favourite plants growing in unrestrained harmony. The simple beauty of the Iceland poppy* (Papaver nudicaule) *is accentuated when planted* en masse.

OPPOSITE: *There is great charm in semi-concealment: much of the appeal is the mystery of what lies beyond. Paths are perhaps the most important feature in the cottage garden — here the path is flanked by cottage favourites, pink valerian and feverfew, and overhung by japonica* (Chaenomeles).

garden. Self-seeding is rampant with carpets of forget-me-nots, love-in-a-mist, honesty, poppies and cosmos running riot through the beds.

Traditionally herbs and vegetables have been included in the cottage garden and these tend to add to the charm, lending an air of practicality to the garden. Certainly herbs such as chives, parsley, bergamot, lemon balm and thyme could only enhance a garden, whilst a few tomato plants and clumps of carrots or lettuce would give added interest as well as having a culinary use. This utilitarian approach to gardening often gives preference to fruit or nut trees for shade. These

are often overlooked in the beauty stakes and are strictly relegated to the orchard or kitchen garden. But many are worth more than a cursory glance. The quince tree (*Cydonia*) is one of the most under-rated trees and is superb throughout the seasons — in spring it resembles a large dogwood with its abundant display of single pale blossoms, followed by a handsome canopy of attractive downy leaves. In autumn, the quince tree is among the last of the trees to lose its leaves, and does so in splendid manner, before baring a handsome winter trunk. An admirable tree in any garden. Other productive trees suit-

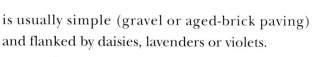

ABOVE: *This miner's cottage with its bull-nose iron verandah is perfectly complemented by the cottage-style garden of roses, lavenders and daisies.*

RIGHT: *The unconstrained nature of the cottage garden is perfect for those who love the old-fashioned shrub roses with their abundance of blooms and fragrance. Lavender is a reliable stalwart with its wonderfully perfumed stalks and pleasing form and foliage throughout winter.*

OPPOSITE: *The abundantly flowering salvias are very much part of the cottage garden. The tall blue flowering* Salvia uliginosa *flowers prolifically throughout late summer and autumn, as does the red* Salvia grahamii *and the deep pink valerian.*

able for the cottage garden are walnut, almond, apple, pear, plum, hazelnut, cherry, mulberry, fig, apricot, nectarine and peach. Berries can be grown over a fence for support, providing ample summer fruit.

Although there is no formal planting scheme or design, this style of garden can be made more interesting by the addition of a little formal symmetry, softened by informal planting, with flowers spilling over on to pathways masking the demarcation between lawn and garden. The only set feature of the cottage garden is the front path, leading from front gate to front door. This

is usually simple (gravel or aged-brick paving) and flanked by daisies, lavenders or violets.

Cottage gardeners seem to have an innate sense of design, skills that are inborn rather than professionally taught. Colour and fragrance are great loves of the cottager, however, neat stripes of gaudy annuals or the newest hybrid roses planted in bare beds bordered with cement edges can create such an effect of orderliness as to lose the cottage effect. Topiary, on the other hand, for all its pretension, is used in a light-hearted manner in the cottage garden and adds a certain touch of whimsy.

LEFT: *The typical cottage garden with picket fence, old-fashioned roses, lavenders, daisies and valerian.*

OPPOSITE: *The simplicity of the country garden can be adapted to the town garden, as in the orchard of this rambling country village garden. Sheep add much to the atmosphere as well as keeping the grass down.*

Architecture can be used to great advantage and to create wonderful supports for various types of climbers. Rose arbours, simple walkways, sundials, bird baths and all manner of garden seating can add appeal if used judiciously.

Fencing needs to be rustic and simple — wooden pickets, dry stone walls or hedging. Tapestry hedging appeals to the true cottage gardener as here there is the opportunity to create a picturesque 'living' fence. A tapestry hedge can be created on an established hedge and will provide year-round interest with the autumn colouring of Virginia creeper, the winter flowering of *Viburnum tinus* or honeysuckle, the early spring blossom of clematis and a profusion of scent, colour and flowers for the house with a perpetual flowering rambling rose, such as 'Mermaid' or 'New Dawn'.

Traditionally, many of our simple garden notions stem from William Robinson, the most influential garden writer of the nineteenth century, who set the worldwide trend for 'cottage style' informal planting. Robinson was highly critical of the stiff formality of Victorian carpet bedding and maintained that the charm of the cottage garden was that they 'were seldom bare and never ugly'. He wrote in *The English Flower Garden*: 'Among the things made by man nothing is prettier than an English cottage garden, and they often teach lessons that "great" gardeners should learn.'

Gertrude Jekyll was a friend and disciple of Robinson and drew her ideas largely from the cottage gardens near her home, Munstead Wood.

Her sense of form and colour was discerning, despite her sight difficulties, and she was sound and eloquent enough to convey her perception in her writings. Vita Sackville-West also carried on the Robinson–Jekyll tradition to striking effect at Sissinghurst. She adored the rambling old-fashioned roses and simple perennials which she used skilfully to create a more 'gentrified' cottage garden atmosphere, still followed today.

Both Gertrude Jekyll and Vita Sackville-West's gardening practices were a romanticised concept of the traditional practical cottage garden, which was literally a means of survival for the rural poor. Far from the herbaceous borders popularised by Jekyll, these were a place they could grow vegetables and fruit to support themselves. The influence of these great garden writers has been far-reaching. Their basic ideals have been implemented in all corners of the globe with the addition of indigenous plants lending individuality.

With the current interest in garden restoration, many gardeners are closely echoing earlier garden traditions, but allowing themselves more flexibility by utilising the wide range of native plants now more readily available and which relate so well to the cottage garden theme.

Essentially, cottage gardening, be it native or exotic in style and form, should be inspiring and evocative — an indulgence of our idealistic longings to recapture the gardens of yesteryear. This garden style does not aim to be a work of art, rather a gathering of favoured plants growing in unrestrained harmony.

The ROMANTIC GARDEN

The very essence of romance is uncertainty.

Oscar Wilde, 1854–1900

As uncertainty is the essence of romance, so is mystique the elixir of the romantic garden. Secrecy, seclusion and subtlety are as vital to the romantic retreat as the colour, form and choice, and plant material.

Romantic gardens are most often the gardens of our imagination — the gardens that we unconsciously desire. It is the gardens of our childhood that we recall with such lucid clarity, those uncontrived gardens of delight. In our memories they were always a tapestry of colour and a treasure trove of delight — violets and forget-me-nots carpeting the ground, old wren's nests in the lilac bushes and dandelion chains to be made from the un-manicured lawns. It is from this tapestry of images that the romantic gardener is able to draw.

ABOVE: *Granny's bonnet or columbine* (Aquilegia vulgaris) *is typical of the plants used in the romantic garden, plants which are chosen for their simplicity and muted colours.*

LEFT: *This rustic bridge is made more inviting by the dappled shade and glimpse of what lies beyond. Romantic gardens are never seen in one glance. Paths invite exploration and garden rooms are made by skilful use of plant material.*

A B O V E : *The wistful pose of this Alice in Wonderland statue lends interest to a secluded corner of the garden.*

L E F T : *A blanket of snow lends an instant air of romance to almost any garden, carpeting the ground in crisp white and accentuating features.*

O P P O S I T E : *Gardening is a continuous artistic venture where as much pleasure lies in the creating as in the final picture. To be able to create a garden picture such as this is akin to any great artistic achievement.*

Stephen Lacey writes in *The Startling Jungle* that most memorable garden pictures are conceived in daydreams. 'Romantic gardeners' notebooks are crammed with messages such as "Build pagoda on site of old coal bunker" or "turn terrace into Persian carpet". Whenever we have an idle moment, at the breakfast table, in a bus queue or on a railway station platform, these precious notes are taken out and carefully considered, and eventually a way is found to translate the images from the realms of fantasy to the realms of reality.'

For any who grew up on that enchanting children's classic, Frances Hodgson Burnett's *The Secret Garden*, gardening could never be anything other than romantic. The seeds planted in this secret garden 'grew as if fairies had tended them . . . And the roses — the roses! Rising out of the grass, tangled round the sun-dial, wreathing the tree trunks and hanging from their branches, climbing up the walls and spreading over them with long garlands falling in cascades.' The realms of fantasy are too often far removed from the realms of reality, but while we temper our ardour for all things impossible perhaps one or two images may be brought to life. Most romantic gardeners have a passion for plants and an innate sense of design. Their imaginations are so vivid and uninhibited that they are often able to bring their fantasies to full creation.

A sense of mystery and seclusion is created by enclosing boundaries, fashioning garden

rooms, wreathing walls in scented climbers and carpeting the ground in a tapestry of colour and fragrance. Create a secluded sanctuary, even in the smallest of spaces. Entice the visitor to wander with beguiling glimpses leading deep into the garden. Exclude the outside world and create an inner sense of sanctuary with walls clothed in a canopy of greenery. Hedges can be used creatively to enclose areas and cloistered corners can be enhanced with a rustic garden bench. Arbours, pergolas, urns, subtle statuary, sundials and bird baths all have a place in the romantic garden. However, the effect can be ruined by trying to be too 'tricksy'. Garden architecture should look as though it 'belongs'. The main role of much garden architecture is to draw the eye along a vista or to highlight an area of the garden and so should be chosen with great sensitivity. The whole romantic mood can be destroyed by anomaly.

Plants are skilfully chosen and arranged. Growth is rampant. Rather a profusion of greenery to soothe the nerves than the impact of a rainbow of brilliant hues to assail the senses. Certainly the garden should be planned with ease of maintenance in mind. A 'romantic garden' soon loses all its 'amour' if it becomes a constant battleground. Old-fashioned roses, lavenders, daisies, herbs, forget-me-nots, campanulas, lilacs, scented climbers and fragrant shrubs form the backbone of the romantic garden.

The well-known garden designer, Edna Walling, did much to popularise the romantic

RIGHT: *The freegrowing nature of these lilies and reeds epitomise the essence of natural water gardens where plant selection is careful yet looks wholly uncontrived.*

garden in Australia and New Zealand. Following on in the tradition of Gertrude Jekyll she skilfully wove a tapestry of romance through her garden designs and writings and was one of the first to appreciate the subtle beauty of the Australian flora. Her skilful blending of foliage, creation of garden rooms, use of garden architecture and the distinct magic she wove around her gardens made them an enduring inspiration. 'It is a most elusive thing,' she writes, 'this matter of design in the garden, and it is not always the ardent horti-culturists who achieve the best results. Although they may be able to bring to maturity faultless specimens of the plant world, yet they may fail to make a garden that is restful and refreshing.'

This is so true today with the hordes of landscape designers being churned out of colleges across the country. I see more and more personal gardens becoming almost institution-alised through their vain endeavours. Maybe these gardens have not yet 'come of age' and will

mellow in their maturity. It is their lack of individuality that I bemoan, the enchantment that can often only come from the gardener. Such magic I have seen woven around a number of older gardens that have been tenderly nurtured over the years with a sensitive hand and a limited budget. Let loose the purse strings and gardens can be created on a grand scale, but they rarely achieve the enchantment and subtlety of a truly romantic garden.

Gardening is a continuous artistic venture where dreams become reality. Gardening writer, Stephen Lacey, believes the best place for garden dreamery is the bath! 'Most keen gardeners are incurable romantics . . . and where better for a prolonged and uninterrupted daydream than the bathroom? Within those tiled walls, with catalogues, seed lists and reference books at your elbow and warm soapy water rippling against your chest, imagination can run riot. Gardens become fragments of paradise.'

L E F T :   *The gentle blue haze of forget-me-nots lend a mystical air to the garden in spring.*

B E L O W :   *Erigeron, hydrangeas and clematis add ambience and charm to this large country home.*

The
COUNTRY
GARDEN

*She walks among the loveliness
she made,
Between the apple-blossom and
the water —
She walks among the patterned pied brocade,
Each flower her son and every tree her
daughter*

VITA SACKVILLE-WEST, 1892–1962
The Land

ountry gardens depend so overwhelmingly on the larger setting of the surrounding countryside that this style is rarely achievable in a small city garden. The generous scale of the country garden invites a more informal approach to gardening, with the bones of the garden provided by a rich variety of foliage in the form of towering trees, shrubs and ground covers. The best country gardens are in harmony with their rural backdrop, 'borrowing' rather than shutting out the surrounding landscape. As part of a larger landscape, the overall visage

ABOVE: *The golden yellow sunflower* (Helianthus annuus).

LEFT: *A carpet of china blue forget-me-nots and old-fashioned aquilegia complement this stately bluestone country homestead. Ivy has been allowed to grow up the base of the massive golden ash* (Fraxinus excelsior 'Aurea'), *whose vast canopy provides welcome summer shade.*

ABOVE: *This historic Australian home and garden has little in the way of flowers, relying predominantly on greenery in the form of trees, lawns, evergreen ground covers, and climbing roses and ornamental grape. This lends a restful air to the grounds and precludes excessive upkeep.*

OPPOSITE: *The traditional farmyard with cobbled paths, alyssum and a gaggle of geese.*

of the countryside will greatly influence the mood of the garden.

These 'borrowed landscapes' can so enhance the look of a garden that elimination is worth considering in a mature garden. This can often open up distant vistas and bring the countryside 'into' the garden, making the garden part of the landscape. This also effectively enlarges the garden, giving enormous breadth and scope.

The art lies in blending the two: the gar-

den and the surrounding landscape. The choice of plant materials and natural landscaping materials, such as stone and timber, is paramount. The planting of indigenous trees and shrubs on the perimeter of the garden imperceptibly merges the two. With no abrupt transition, the gradual drift from garden to the muted countryside beyond makes a pleasing picture.

In Australia, the days of shutting out the alien landscape beyond have long gone. Many early Australian settlers perhaps felt threatened

by the unfamiliar territory and so attempted to make an oasis of exotica totally enclosed and separate from the wider landscape. Today Australians fully appreciate the beauty of the natural landscape. These early gardens are historically significant and are often classic works of art. Transposed into our time they serve more as an echo of times past than a modern masterpiece. Strict but sympathetic discipline is needed in the ongoing maintenance of such gardens, which form the basis of much of Australia's gardening heritage.

Within the country garden there are many styles: wild, cottage, native, romantic, old-fashioned, classic or a combination of styles. As a garden reflects the lifestyle and personality of its owner so also should it exist primarily for enjoyment. As much entertaining is done from the home, tennis courts, barbecue and courtyard areas, and swimming pools are often incorporat-

ed within the country garden, along with vegetable gardens, orchards, tree houses, garden sheds, garages and carports, dog kennels and fowl runs. To accommodate all this and yet create a composition totally in harmony, design and layout needs sound consideration.

As the home will be the central pivot of the garden, the style of house, the geography of the surrounding area and any historical significance need contemplation. Whether starting afresh or redesigning an existing garden, it is important to have an overall plan in mind. Winter sun and summer shade, prevailing wind direction, external vistas and practical use areas (clothes line, garage, incinerator, garden shed and compost) are all of primary concern.

British landscape designer John Brookes, advises designing your ideal layout first, before the distraction of planting. As an artist creates a masterpiece, detail is left till last.

While the garden concept must be visually appealing, upkeep must not become a struggle for survival. Achievement of 'the perfect garden' should not be at all costs. While many country gardens retain their traditional size, labour and income have often dwindled. Expectations and planting schemes should be attainable.

Thus a more relaxed style of gardening is called for, one where the charm emanates from a slightly unrestrained and overgrown appearance. Colour harmony can play a large role in the over-all appearance. A slightly disorderly jumble of greenery can have a charm all of its own whereas introducing too many gaudy or conflicting colours can bring the eye to focus too accutely on each particular area. Carpets of bulbs, wide expanses of lawn, perennials rather than annuals and simple ground covers form the basis for the country garden with groupings of simple trees rather than a botanic collection in geometric precision.

Paths, walls and edges blend in harmoniously if created from the natural material of the countryside. Sunken ha-ha walls can effectively merge garden and landscape into one (see page 119). Gravel is also far more sympathetic to the

country garden than stretches of concrete paths. Functional but unattractive outbuildings can be attractively clothed in swags of greenery.

The planting scheme can become more unrestrained as it reaches the boundary with the actual perimeter being camouflaged as much as possible. Simplicity is the key, particularly in the country garden and, for utmost impact, plant *en masse*. A hedge of one species (hawthorn, spiraea, rose, dogwood), a border of one plant (catmint, chamomile, dianthus, viola, candytuft), a group of the same shrubs (*Buddleia*, amalanchier, mock orange, cistus or japonica) or a driveway of the same tree (sycamore, eucalypt, linden, Manchurian pear) will have greater appeal in the larger landscape of the country than a conglomeration of everything. Even within the orchard, the use of one type of bulb to plant in drifts is more alluring than a rainbow of colours.

This simplicity, perhaps the most essential element of the true country garden, can be adapted to the smaller confines of a town garden. In the city garden the garden furniture often sets the tone; to achieve a country look, simple wooden or cane seats have more of a country air than sculptured stone and smartly painted ironwork.

The
FRAGRANT
GARDEN

*If colour is the substance with which
the romantic gardener spins his
magic web, scent is his means of ensuring
that his prey is powerless to escape.*

STEPHEN LACEY,
The Startling Jungle

A garden bereft of fragrance is a garden without a soul. Much of our enjoyment of a garden is heightened by scent, which has rightfully been described as 'the soul of the flower'. Nothing has a greater power to recall visions of childhood or long ago memories. As garden writer, Barbara Damrosch says: 'The scents of plants are like unseen ghosts. They sneak up on you as you round a turn in the garden, before you can see the plants from which they came.' This is very much part of their elusiveness. To round a corner or walk down a path and suddenly breathe in the faint aroma of a plant creates the delight of finding the source. This intangible fragrance adds another whole dimension to gardening and our enjoyment of it.

ABOVE: *Roses conjure the notion of fragrance as few other plants do and one of the most enchanting fragrant roses is 'The Reeve'. This cupped form is typical of the David Austin Roses.*

LEFT: *Old-fashioned shrub roses, poppies and violets provide an enchanting spring display.*

ABOVE: *A closer inspection of the classic beauty of this aged sundial reveals the subtle scent from the roses planted in the sunken circular rose garden.*

LEFT: *The fragrant subtle beauty of wisteria. The pendulous, sweetly-scented flowers are borne in clusters during early spring.*

OPPOSITE: *Originally a kitchen garden, old-fashioned scented roses and lavenders have been added to this walled courtyard garden. The fragrance heightens awareness of the plants, thereby adding to the allure.*

It is not such a bizarre notion to plant a garden for scent alone. As hybridisation gives us larger, gaudier flowers, we tend to look back to the plants from our childhood — the older varieties that would literally make your head swim with their fragrance. There is no limit to the scope of scented plants, and when planning a fragrant garden, there is no need to sacrifice design, colour, scale or style. It is just as possible to have a scented wildflower or native garden as a scented cottage garden. Even the utilitarian kitchen garden may become a fragrant oasis with rosemary and lavender border hedges and the sweet scent of strawberries mingling with the scent of ripe tomatoes.

Herb gardens are a scented garden within themselves. And we need not be too fatuous about our lawns: aromatic lawns, which have been used since early Tudor times, can create a wonderful atmosphere in areas of little traffic.

Although herb lawns are not entirely practicable for widespread use, a small area carpeted with lemon-scented thyme (*Thymus citriodorus)* would provide fragrance in abundance, leaves for the kitchen and a minimum care, evergreen ground cover.

Few plants conjure such notions of fragrance as old-fashioned roses. The rich fragrance of *Rosa eglanteria*, reminiscent of fresh green apples; Félicité Parmentier with its scent of honeysuckle; the wonderful climber, *Rosa filipes* 'Kiftsgate' with its mass of powerfully fragrant single white flowers; the double white banksia rose with its distinct violet fragrance; and the rich damask scent of Omar Khayyam.

In my garden, I never fail to be amazed by the almost overpowering scent from an old bush of winter honeysuckle (*Lonicera fragrantissima*). Even approaching the garden at some distance or when under a blanket of snow, I am lured by the

delicate lemon scent. Another altogether enticing fragrance is that of the old-fashioned rambling rose, Madame Alfred Carrière. Clambering up the old stone wall in our courtyard, I am unable to pass without burying my nose into one of the many blush-cream cupped blooms that are so prolifically produced.

A walk in the bush or countryside is another experience altogether. Who is able to resist taking a eucalyptus leaf or a piece of wild heather to crush between your fingers for that wonderful scent that is strong enough to make your eyes water. It is surely the scent that lingers longest in our memories and can be so quickly brought back to life by simply throwing a few dried leaves on an open fire, or even a leaf in the teapot. The sweet scent of lavender conjures up the farmlands of rural France in summertime while the mint bush (*Prostanthera*) may bring back memories of alpine walks. However, nothing rivals the overwhelming scent of the lemon-scented gum (*Eucalyptus citriodora*). I have seen this planted with stunning success in a winding country driveway in Australia.

There is no set formula for planning a scented garden — it can be as simple as a win-dow-box, balcony or courtyard of terracotta pots full to overflowing with scented plants, as vast as a wild country garden or as extensive as a large forest or bushland domain. In essence, a scented garden is a personal collection of special plants, all selected with fragrance as the number one priority, without disregarding texture, form, harmony, colour or height. Guy Acloque from Alderley Grange in England says 'when planning an aromatic garden, always remember to plant with profusion and never confusion'. This is true of many styles of gardening, but it is essential in the fragrant garden where scents should complement, not conflict.

With our constant preoccupation with visual images, scent is often overlooked. However, fragrance is the very spirit of the garden and one that can give the greatest pleasure. As Stephen Lacey says: 'Its inclusion can transform the character of the scheme, giving it an extra dimension with which to stimulate the senses and activate the imagination.'

Fragrance is heightened in enclosed areas, and a courtyard is an ideal area for a miniature scented garden. Enclosed areas can also be created with the use of scented hedges or by cov-

ering walls with fragrant climbers. These give the illusion of mystery and seclusion. Narrow paths encourage perfumes to be released on passing and scented ground covers spilling onto the pathway emit wondrous fragrances if stepped on when passing by.

Night-scented plants such as the tall white tobacco and evening primrose add another dimension to a fragrant garden and are ideally placed along a verandah that is used on balmy evenings or under an open bedroom window on warm evenings.

Interestingly enough, it is pastel and white flowers that are among the most fragrant, with the orange and scarlet shades providing the least scent. In order of potency, pale pink heads the list, moving through the mauves and yellows to the less scented purples and blues.

The idea of a scented garden is not merely to induce one outdoors — great pleasure can be had from bringing the garden inside. If you have ever been to hospital it is possible to appreciate the breath of fresh air that comes with a sweet scented posy or, when away from home, from a vase of flowers on the bedside table. Then there is the simple pleasure of evoking those springtime-summer scents all year round with potpourris, bath bags or scented linen closets.

The
WILD
GARDEN

How elusive that sweet disorder.

The trend towards a more relaxed type of gardening has focused attention back on the 'sweet disorder' of the wild garden. Traditionally, the wild garden was only one component of the entire garden, however, the appeal of such an uninhibited style of gardening is attracting many gardeners to use this style solely.

True wild gardening is gardening as nature would have it — no confines, pretence or inhibitions. Plants are allowed to naturalise, self-seeding in unlikely spots without notions of placement, colour co-ordination or height. The massed profusion eliminates weeding and gives a feeling of living tapestry.

This relaxed informality is not only labour saving but illuminates the whole concept of the 'wild garden'. Here nature takes a hand and artificiality is eased away. The essence lies in creating an uncontrived look, a feeling of peace and restfulness.

ABOVE: *Teasel* (Dipsacus fullonum) *is a favourite of bees and dried flower enthusiasts.*

LEFT: *Aptly named 'the fairy tale walk', this age-old secret pathway is carpeted with leaves from the viburnums, privet and wild grape, and is flanked with native violets.*

L E F T :   *William Robinson, that great advocate of the wild garden wrote in his classic book* The Wild Garden *'never show the naked earth: clothe it'. Forget-me-nots (*Myosotis*) are one of the most prolific self-seeders, filling in bare patches and carpeting the ground with a sea of china blue flowers.*

There are two schools of thought on the design and care of the wild garden. William Robinson, the founder of the wild garden concept, wrote: 'The owner might go away for ten years and find it more beautiful than ever on his return.' For anyone who has read Frances Hodgson-Burnett's delightful children's classic, *The Secret Garden*, this romanticised vision of the beauty of a garden locked away for years echoes Robinson's sentiments entirely. Gertrude Jekyll on the other hand, while writing on the delights of wild gardening believed 'no kind of gardening is so difficult to do well, or is so full of pitfalls and of paths of peril'.

Penelope Hobhouse goes one step further, deterring all but true stalwarts to the cause: 'These "wild" gardens need to be as carefully composed as an artist's paint on a canvas, with an eye to heights, shapes, density and colour . . . it should be [as] carefully planned and executed as any formal pattern and actually requires more aesthetic and horticultural skill.'

The wild garden came into being in the nineteenth century, a time when navigators explored uncharted seas and countries, returning with vast collections of plants from afar, which were then acclimatised, naturalised and distributed far and wide. Through travel to other countries, gardeners sought to emulate the Renaissance gardens of Italy and France. Formality was at its peak. Topiary, sculpture, geometric beds and glasshouse gardening was the rage. Great

ABOVE: *'A host of golden daffodils' naturalised in a wild country garden. Drifts of daffodils have more appeal than rigid lines. Try filling a bucket with bulbs, throwing them out by the handful, and planting each one where it lands.*

LEFT: *No contrived planting to spoil the natural flow of trees and water. These elms have been allowed to naturalise, carpeting the ground with a thick layer of leaf mulch which takes care of itself — no mowing, watering or weeding is required. In autumn, the ground is a golden carpet; in winter the leaves are grey and crisp; in spring the ground is scattered with fallen elm blossom; and in summer the dappled shade provides welcome relief from the midday sun.*

emphasis was placed on bright colours in the flower beds. 'Bedding out' was widely practised, emphasising colour to the exclusion of everything else. The form of plant was of less importance than the impact of its colour — no subtle harmonies. The bedding out gardener aimed to have everything in full colour *all* the time!

A new school of thought was developing at this time, led by William Robinson, who consistently rebelled against the current gardening practices in favour of a more natural look. Through his magazine articles, editorials, essays, and books (eighteen written between 1868 and 1924) he championed the English cottage gardens with their lack of formality and emphasis on individual plants. He wrote long and often on the

joys of wild gardening, condemning pretentious gardening principles and architecture. Needless to say, he set the garden dignitaries of the day on their heads, encouraging ways of escape from 'the death-note of the pastry-cook's garden' deploring their 'pastry-work gardening'.

His classic book, *The Wild Garden* (1870), is still topical today, attacking the formal artificiality of high Victorian gardens and passionately advocating the planting of wild and native plants.

Robinson's cause was helped by world influences. During the latter half of the nineteenth century, philosophers, artists, writers and poets were coming to appreciate nature as a benign rather than a hostile force. The old cry of

ABOVE: *The magic of snow — a driveway of elms is transformed*
with a   dusting of snow.

A B O V E :   *There is nothing contrived in the wild garden — leaves are left to carpet the ground and fencing is rustic and unpretentious.*

William Kent 'that nature abhors a straight line' was replaced by a principle of the new picturesque school, 'nature abhors hard edges', a maxim widely held today.

The Robinsonian school of thought led to the belief that the typical garden should become a place 'dedicated to the honourable pleasures of rejoicing the eye, refreshing the nose and renewing the spirit'. This approach to gardening soon made its way to Australia. For many early Australian settlers, the environment was foreign and harsh, and they quickly tried to make it look as English as possible. Early paintings show how the native vegetation was completely overlooked. The native eucalypts were too subtle in their form and beauty to be appreciated.

It was not until Edna Walling and William Guilfoyle started incorporating 'wild gardens' within their designs that Australians started to form an appreciation of their native flora. Guilfoyle believed the Australian wild garden should *not* be an imitation of those made in England and should, instead, be enriched with our unique horticultural abundance. In this way, he incorporated much of the native vegetation together with bulbs from South Africa, shrubs from New

Zealand and many other subtropical plants from around the globe.

Edna Walling, who carried many of the Jekyll–Robinson gardening principles with her from England to Australia, also widely extolled the use of native plants. Many of her large garden designs incorporated a 'wild' area to offset the formal garden. This was executed with stunning effect, although there are precious few examples remaining today.

Native or exotic, or a mixture of both, nature's practice of covering the earth's surface in profusion is carried out in the wild garden: leaves are of more importance than the flowers; foliage blends together without creating disharmony; and there are no garish colours or exotic variegateds.

Design is best kept simple, creating a feeling of enclosure with sweeping curves and broad groupings of plants. In the wild garden, more than any other area, greatest effect is gained in using repetition. Whether it be a sweep of bluebells or a mat of everlasting daisies, the overall appearance will be greatly enhanced and unified by a recurring theme.

This is not really the garden for the plantsman. Single plants that draw attention to themselves are out of place, as are tender imports that will need extra coddling to keep alive. As Gertrude Jekyll warns: 'Wild gardening should never look like garden gardening, or, as it so sadly often does, like garden plants gone astray.'

Nature is the best guide in the arrangement of plants. As Robinson believed, the 'common sin' of wild garden planting was overdoing. 'To scatter narcissi equally over the grass everywhere is to destroy all chances of repose, of relief, and of seeing them in the ways in which they

often arrange themselves.' He talked of looking to the way wild plants arrange themselves or even the way clouds group together in the sky.

Edna Walling's method of achieving natural planting groups was to fill a bucket with potatoes, literally fling these out with abandon, and plant a tree or bulb wherever a potato landed. Once established, the plants will soon begin to naturalise. In larger gardens, this method can be carried out effectively in the orchard, where in spring time the fruit blossom is picturesquely complemented by flowering bulbs *en masse*.

John Codrington, the venerable globe-trotting garden designer, is someone close to my own heart. Describing his own garden as 'quite wild and mad' he decided to put the record straight after many people, including Penelope Hobhouse, had said such 'nice' things about his garden in their books. So, writing to *The Garden*

(the journal of the Royal Horticultural Society) he stated that his garden compares to others 'as an uncouth, ragamuffin gypsy does to the perfect bowler-hatted, briefcase carrying city gent!'

The very essence of the wild garden is that although the environment can be controlled, the art lies in making the methods of control look natural. As a collaboration between art and nature, this type of garden is neither constrained nor contrived. While aspect, climate, soil type and texture, rainfall and situation will all affect the result, the over-riding influence is the personality of the gardener. It takes a certain misty-eyedness to be able to appreciate the gentle 'untidiness' of a wild garden. Edna Wallings' quote 'there was an air of wildness about the garden. It was the sort of garden in which you could garden if you wanted to but if you didn't it would not matter', philosophises the essence of wild gardening.

The HERB GARDEN

Speak not — whisper not:
Here groweth thyme and bergamot;
Dark-spiked rosemary and myrrh
Lean stalked, purple lavender.

WALTER DE LA MARE, 1873–1956
The Sunken Garden

Herbs are among the most enchanting and easy to grow of all garden plants and as such, make the contemplation of designing a separate herb garden a delightful prospect. Wonderfully fragrant, colourful and flavourful, herbs are rightfully reclaiming the popularity they occupied in mediaeval times.

There is something romantic about creating a 'herb' garden as distinct from the garden proper. A special area, specifically planted to these culinary delights is certainly far more whimsical and easy than the slog of a vegetable garden, for all its culinary practicality.

The herb garden is one area where it is possible to create horticultural works of art with garden knots or

A B O V E : *A rare white form of borage* (Borago officinalis) *which self-seeds and flowers as prolifically as the blue variety.*

L E F T : *Old garden implements hang on the garden shed wall behind an old bathtub overflowing with herbs and nasturtiums and the purple ball-head of chive flowers in the foreground.*

intricate garden tapestry designs of hedges and paths, without looking out of place within the scale of the garden. In a more informal garden, randomly placed groupings of herbs can look equally attractive with their potpourri of colour and fragrance. Even a pot of chives on a window-sill or a group of terracotta pots filled to over-flowing with mint, basil, chives, thyme, rosemary and parsley at the kitchen door can look refreshingly appealing.

So ancient is the use for herbs that they are inseparably linked with nostalgia for times gone past when the lady of the house spent enchanted hours gathering bundles of herbs to take into the still-room. Today we grow them, if not for medicinal or cosmetic purposes, for cook-ing at least. Most gardeners unconsciously use herbs in their gardens — take away the lavenders, rosemary, chamomiles, thymes, santolina and nas-turtiums and many of our favourite garden plants are gone.

Herbs are among my most treasured gar-den plants. There is little that can compare with the simplicity, form and scent of a lavender or rosemary hedge; the luxury of stepping on a thyme lawn or the brilliance of a bergamot flower. Their tapestry of colour, form, texture and fragrance remain virtually unrivalled.

Their usefulness is infinite. A simple bunch of mint does wonders in an ice cold tumb-ler of water while a more sophisticated blend of basil and tarragon can provide a tasty substitute for many of the chemical and artificial additives that are so often used to add piquancy to dishes. Herbs bring out the best in foods, enhancing flavours and giving a lift to the simplest dishes.

A B O V E : *An old metal watering can is valued as much for its decorative appeal as for its usefulness.*

L E F T : *The well-defined layout of this herb garden is deceptively simple. Clipped box hedging, brick paving, thyme and a weathered sundial give the appearance of agelessness, and yet this garden has only just been established.*

Herb vinegars and oils, mustards, sorbets, jellies, breads, cheeses, sauces and teas are among the many culinary uses.

Potpourris, sachets, wreaths, bouquets, nosegays or tussie mussies bring the colour and fragrance of the garden indoors and provide beauty and fragrance in the dreariest of places. Bunches of lavender are an age-old recipe for keeping the moths at bay in the linen cupboard as well as providing beautifully fragrant sheets. Herbs for drying should be picked early in the day after the dew has dried. Ideally they are at their best just before they bloom or as the flower buds open. They can be hung head-downwards in bunches or spread to dry on racks in a dry well-ventilated position. Hung from beams in the kitchen, herbs can give a wonderful country air to any city home. I have seen the simplest hand-made twig rack hung from a kitchen ceiling used to dry herbs most effectively.

Medicinally, herbs have been used since the ancient Egyptians and are now having increasing value amongst pharmacologists. Herbal potions are finding new respect among a society that is becoming wary and immune to many modern medicines. Part of their charm lies in the folklore and ancient knowledge handed down through the generations.

Herbs are the easiest of plants to grow. They will grow in most soils, flourishing in poor or gravelly soil. Their one prerequisite is full sun, although there are some that will survive in a damp and shady position. The most important consideration in planning a herb garden is easy accessibility. A sprint over a wet lawn for a sprig of parsley is not as conducive as a plot (or pot) at

the kitchen door. Many herbs make attractive
edging plants along paths, or can be used in the
herbaceous border for those more adventurous.
Low-growing thymes and pennyroyal can be
added to the rock garden or planted in cracks in
the paving. If space is really a problem, hanging
baskets of herbs can be an attractive as well as
practical solution.

Herbs can be grown with charming abandon in the informal herb garden. Planted
closely together, they will form an impressionistic
riot of greenery and fragrance. This glorious dis-
array can hold appeal to the gardener that does
not like the uniformity and rigidity of the classical
herb garden. As many of the herbs are prolific
self-seeders (parsley, borage, lavender, dill, fennel
and lemon balm), gardening can be through
elimination rather than planting.

The sense of symmetry and balance in the
traditional herb garden is especially pleasing to
the eye, and can provide just the touch of formality needed in a large garden. When contemplating such artistry as intricate knot gardens or
parterre gardens, it is infinitely helpful to draw a
detailed plan on graph paper or in scale on art
paper, before rushing into the actual planting.
Beds can be separated by paths of gravel, lawn or
brick and can be edged with low-growing thymes
or, for a more formal effect, with a clipped hedge
such as lavender, rosemary or santolina. In the
formal garden, plants look best if kept trimmed
so that the outline of the plan remains distinct. A
central feature such as a sundial, bird bath, dovecote, piece of statuary or bee skep gives an added
touch of formality.

Where space is limited or garden beds are
minimal, a herbal walk can be an interesting concept. This can be as simple and practical as a path
edged with parsley, chives and thyme or, for
greater effect, it can be more formally planted
with clipped lavenders, of which there are many
varieties, to provide a major axis within the gar-

den. A white lavender hedge for example can provide the perfect foil for almost any other plant, be it herb, native or exotic.

To add interest to the service area of the garden, the clothes line area could be paved with large slate pavers or even bricks in a circular pattern and herbs could be grown in the cracks. The whole area could then be hedged with a fragrant herb or even a variety of mints. Normally so intrusive in the garden proper, the mints could safely merge into the lawn and be mown at the outer perimeter.

Personal herb collections can be as many and varied as their owners, ranging from Shakespearean, biblical, medicinal, cosmetic, culinary, colonial or even sleep-inducing herbs! Many herbs are also used for companion planting, to improve the flavour of some vegetables and to allay pests and diseases.

While many gardeners plant garlic or the daintier garlic chives at the base of their roses to deter aphids, garlic can also help deter leaf curl on peach trees and will discourage many common insects in the orchard and kitchen garden. A hedge of garlic around the entire garden will even deter rabbits! The strong scent of rue, tansy and pennyroyal repels flies and if snakes are a problem, try lad's love! If mice, rats or ants are a problem, mint is said to deter them while rue will keep cats and even dogs at bay. Many herbs have great affinity with vegetables: chamomile is a good companion to onions and cabbage; tomatoes with basil; strawberries and borage grow happily together; and comfrey is the wonder herb in the compost bin, activating the whole compost process.

One of the great pleasures in a herb garden is the lasting perfume of its plants. To pick a leaf and squeeze it between your fingers is to breathe in the heady aroma. This is particularly piquant after a shower of rain or on a clear still evening after watering.

The ROSE GARDEN

Loveliest of lovely things are they,
On earth that soonest pass away.
The rose that lives its little hour
Is prized beyond the sculptured flower

WILLIAM CULLEN BRYANT, 1794–1878

For pure atmosphere and fragrance, a garden of old roses is unrivalled. Combining tangible beauty and an intoxicating scent with a romantic history, roses are truly the queen of flowers.

Much of their charm lies in their romantic history: the Red Rose of Lancaster is thought to have been first cultivated as long ago as 3000 BC; Damascena Versicolor was named in 1551 to commemorate the English War of the Roses; and Souvenir de la Malmaison was bred in 1843 and named after Empress Josephine's rose garden at Malmaison. It has been said that when Marie Antoinette entered France to be married to the Dauphin, she was

ABOVE: *This richly fragrant climbing rose, Wedding Day, is a mass of small single white blooms midsummer.*

LEFT: *This rustic summerhouse has been planted with fragrant climbing roses. The pale pink rose is New Dawn, one of the most popular of the pink-flowering climbing roses with its prolific recurrent flowering habit and sweet fragrance.*

ABOVE: Rosa rugosa *is a fragrant single rose with large decorative hips.*

LEFT: *A green–white colour predominance provides a restful cool atmosphere during the heat of midsummer. Gloire Lyonnaise flowers against a background of* Kolkwitzia *(beauty bush) and provides dappled shade to the Solomon's seal bulbs growing at the base of the rose.*

OPPOSITE: *This sunken rose garden has been filled with an abundance of fragrant standard roses, providing a sea of colour and a mass of blooms for picking.*

preceded by the maidens of the town of Provens where she stayed, with a bed of rose petals. She was never seen without a rose on her head and carried the bloom towards her face as she spoke, it is said to cover certain dental deficiencies! Sissinghurst Castle is an old gallica discovered by Vita Sackville-West growing in her garden at Sissinghurst Castle while the pink damask, Omar Khayyam, was raised by seeds collected from the bush growing over his grave in Nashapur, Iran.

Such names invoke much of their charm, but charisma aside, their great vigour, resistance to disease , fragrance, hardiness and choice of habit add much to their reputation. Their tolerance to a wide range of soils, sites and uses make them great assets in home landscaping, and while preferring full sun, some, like Mme Legras de St Germain are tolerant to semi-shade. They will grow quite happily amongst other small trees, shrubs and ground cover plants and many of the old roses need precious little pruning. You only have to look at some old deserted cottages to see century-old plantings of suprisingly healthy roses blooming away quite unaided. Pruning out the

ABOVE: *One of the beauties of the rose world, Constance Spry is a large spreading shrub with abundant paeony-like cupped blooms throughout summer.*

RIGHT: *Many roses are wonderfully suited to growing in pots, such as this charming David Austin rose, Dame Prudence, which only grows to just over half a metre in height. A pink flowering prostrate thyme spills over the edge of the terracotta pot.*

dead or unproductive old wood is often all that is needed to revitalise neglected plants.

It has been said by rose enthusiasts that there is no landscaping requirement that cannot be solved with a rose. The common misconception of the old roses is that they have only one flowering (as do most garden shrubs) and that they can be unsightly during winter. However, just as there are evergreen roses, so are there thornless varieties, perpetual bloomers, groundhugging, clambering and climbing ramblers, and weeping standards. Rose arches, arbours, screens, pergolas and hedges are more formal ways of using roses, but roses are just as effective for clothing unsightly buildings and fences, clambering up old trees or propping up the old garden or tool shed.

Gertrude Jekyll devotes a chapter to 'Roses for converting ugliness to beauty' in one of her books. 'What a splendid exercise it would be if people would only go round their places and look for all the ugly corners, and just think how they might be made beautiful by the use of free-growing Roses,' she writes so convincingly.

There are two distinct types of gardeners — those that prefer the pruned modern specimens planted geometrically in formal garden beds, or those who prefer the rambling, overgrown look of the fragrant old roses. Either way, there are manifold species to chose from. Great pleasure can be derived from going beyond the everyday nursery varieties and looking for the rarer, more precious varieties. While everyone knows the Iceberg, yellow banksia and Dorothy Perkins, there are hundreds of varieties to chose from that will give your garden individuality.

Many roses are easy to grow from cuttings — perhaps this is the reason for the popularity of the banksia and Iceberg roses. Tip cuttings put into sand will almost unfailingly bring forth new rose bushes. There is great anticipation in striking an unknown rose and waiting for its first bud to unfold. Old rose enthusiasts are often fascinated by the hardy old roses growing in many graveyards, some surviving unaided for well over a hundred years. There can be much satisfaction in naming and identifying many of these true heritage roses.

Perhaps much of the appeal of a rose garden is the infinite variety from which to choose: the opulent, globular cabbage roses or the striking large single roses with prominent stamens; the dainty miniature roses or the vigorous ramblers; and the portlands, mosses, bourbons, musks, rugosas, damasks, gallicas, china and boursalt roses.

Rose garden designs can be as simple or complex as required. A rose garden without any other interest can be a dull affair, so it is worth seeking complementary plants to provide year-round interest. Lilies, *Alchemilla mollis*, delphiniums, *Erigeron*, violets, campanulas, gypsophila, foxgloves, candytuft, columbines, lavenders, daisies, hellebores, bulbs and box edging are among the many plants that can add interest to the rose garden. The soft white or pastels of these plants complement and intensify the charm of the rose.

ABOVE: *This flamboyant and floriferous climber, Mme Gregoire Staechlin (Spanish Beauty) has been used here to great effect as a 'swag'. Its rich fragrance, long and early flowering period, and prolific crop of pear-shaped fruit in autumn make it a much treasured rose.*

ROSES SUITABLE FOR HEDGING: Penelope, Boule de Neige, Honeyflow, Madame Plantier, Moonbeam, *Rosa rugosa alba*, Cornelia.

GROUND COVERING ROSES: Paulii, Nozomi, *Macrantha*, *Wichuraiana* (Memorial rose), Pearl Drift, Sea Foam, Max Graf.

CLIMBING ROSES: Blossomtime, Milkmaid, New Dawn, Aimee Vibert, Nancy Hayward, *Rosa filipes* 'Kiftsgate', Prioress, Apple Blossom, Mme Alfred Carriere.

EVERGREEN ROSES: Banksia (white and yellow — double and single), Wedding Day, *Bracteata*

(Macartney Rose), Silver Moon, Mme Alfred Carrière, Mermaid, Iceberg, Laevigata (Cherokee Rose), *Wichuriana* (Memorial rose).

SCENTED ROSES: Mme Hardy, Mme Legras de Saint Germain, Kathleen Harrop, La Reine Victoria, Mme Isaac Pereire, Stanwell Perpetual, Devoniensis.

FAVOURITE BEDDING ROSES: Souvenir de St Anne's, Dainty Bess, Constance Spry, Shropshire Lass, Chaucer, Carabella, Schneezwerg, The Wife of Bath, Wild Flower, Pax.

PERPETUAL FLOWERING ROSES: Souvenir de Philemon Cochet, Golden Wings, Louise Odier, Frau Karl Druschki, Grüss an Aachen, Clair Matin.

The COURTYARD GARDEN

*I do not envy the owners of
very large gardens.*

GERTRUDE JEKYLL, 1843–1932

T he subtle pleasure of courtyard gardening has been underestimated in the quest for vaster, more expansive gardens. The lush greenery, dappled shade, privacy and cool paving of a courtyard area add a whole new dimension to any home or garden and can be one of the most pleasing gardens to relax in. Having lived with a courtyard, in both temperate and cool climates, it would be hard to survive without. Providing not only a private outdoor living area they serve as a shady oasis in summer and a sun trap in winter. If designed to catch morning sun, they then provide some shelter from the full midday sun.

Size is of less consequence than the overall aesthetic appeal, although the more intimate the area, the greater the charm. There are no hard and fast rules for courtyard

ABOVE: *The sparse elegance of this courtyard garden complements a magnificent harbour view. The row of clipped* Buxus *in washed terracotta pots provides the perfect touch of formality.*

LEFT: *Waterlilies soften the form of the pond in this enclosed courtyard. The textured white trunks of the silver birches (Betula pendula) add height without dominating the scene. The pale* Clematis montana *drapes itself over the walls and balustrade giving an unparalleled display in spring.*

ABOVE: *Courtyard arrangements can be kept sparse for maximum effect as in this city garden where the elegance of a tall standard* Buxus *is a strong enough statement to stand alone.*

RIGHT: *A solitary silver birch* (Betula pendula) *allows filtered sunlight into this small rectangular courtyard. The trailing aluminium plant* (Pilea cadierei) *softens the base of the enchanting sculpture, which is in perfect proportion to the pond. Ivy, pilea and acanthus provide year-round greenery along the back wall.*

OPPOSITE *In this large country courtyard, herbs are grown for use in the nearby kitchen.*

planting although it is wise to lean towards evergreen plants rather than those that flower spectacularly for a week or so a year and then look stark and untidy for the remainder. Courtyards provide a micro-climate for growing, providing a long growing season and luxuriant growth. However, before smothering every available wall in greenery, consider the charm of whitewashed walls or the warm earthy washes associated with Mediterranean courtyards.

Colours are best kept to a minimum as restfulness is the aim. Green and white are the coolest colours and the soft smoky green of many herbs and Australian plants can also go towards creating a restful retreat. Lawn is rarely feasible but there is a vast range of stone, brick or terracotta tiling to choose from.

Courtyards need furnishing: tables, chairs, pots and lots of greenery will give the area individuality and provide an outdoor entertaining or recreation area. Linking the house to the garden, courtyards provide a restful private sanctuary to look on to from rooms looking out to the area. In many townhouses, the courtyard is the only area available for gardening.

Such is their versatility and attractiveness that it is hard to imagine architects not utilising courtyards more. From the smallest inner city home to the sprawling country homestead, there are untold advantages. As Edna Walling writes in

ABOVE: *The focus of this courtyard garden is the waterlily-covered pond which enhances the tranquil nature of the garden.*

OPPOSITE: *Seats or benches are an important component of the courtyard garden and look particularly effective, as here, in a combination of wrought iron and wood.*

her *Book of Australian Garden Design*: 'To look through doorways and windows on to freshgreen foliage, into shady courtyards, and on to cool, clean paving, is to live comfortably and gently in summer. Trees, cloisters, courtyards and pergola-covered terraces give an hospitable and expansive air to the small house, inviting one to walk out into the open rather than to remain cooped up in it for fear of the blistering sun that sometimes beats upon its very walls.'

Fragrance is heightened in an enclosed area and can be used to full advantage in the courtyard garden. The hardy evergreen climber *Clematis armandii* is superb on walls or lattice with the pink and white star flowers of apple blossom or pure white saucer-shaped flowers of snow drift providing fragrance and elegance. The native Australian jasmines (*Jasminum suavissimum, lineariis, calcareum, racemosum* or *simplicifolium*) are attractive climbers with delicate star-shaped flowers. The evergreen *Daphne pontica* with its

pale green, lemon-scented flowers sweetens the air late winter and early spring.

Plant combinations are endless. For the herb enthusiast, potted standard bays, French lavender, topiary rosemary in pots, saucers brimming with apple mint and lemon balm, tubs filled with chives, thyme growing amongst the paving and a potpourri of basil, tarragon, parsley, borage and oregano will serve as culinary aids while providing a tranquil outdoor planting scheme. Australian plant enthusiasts can choose bird-attracting plants like the lemon-scented tea-tree (*Leptospermum petersonii*) with its fresh lemon-scented foliage said also to repel mosquitoes; *Angophora cordifolia; Clematis aristata;* the native wax flower (*Eriostemon myoporoides*); melaleucas; and banksias or acacias along with a pool of water or bird bath to bring birds into their courtyard. Romanticists may choose to smother the walls in old world roses or group together pots of standard roses, topiary honeysuckle and box, lavenders, hydrangeas, campanulas, daisies, and species camellias perhaps complemented by a cast iron marble-topped table and a scattering of chairs and benches. Choosing a certain colour combination can add interest and flow on from the colours used to decorate the interior of the home. A grey and white courtyard, using grey foliage plants with white flowers, can be elegant and restful, while blue and white is a perennial favourite. The soft mauves of wisteria, lavenders, Persian lilac, hydrangeas and catmint have a certain restfulness about them while a courtyard planted purely for fragrance has great appeal.

The inclusion of trees in a courtyard setting depends largely on the scale of the area. A large deciduous tree providing dappled summer shade and winter sun can be a feature whilst a sitting area sheltered by an ornamental grape (*Vitus vinifera*) serves the same purpose. A water feature in the courtyard can add a touch of tranquillity.

The
KITCHEN
GARDEN

Much as I love the flower garden and the
woodland, I am by no means indifferent
to the interest and charm of the kitchen
garden. For though its products are for the
most part utilitarian, they all have their
life-histories and on the rare occasions
when I am free to take a quiet stroll for
pure pleasure of the garden,
I often take it among the vegetables.

GERTRUDE JEKYLL, 1843–1932

There is something immensely pleasing about the kitchen garden with its tidy orderliness. Although not planted for pure aesthetic allure, its appeal lies in its wonderful sense of productivity. There is also much pleasure in the individuality of design and layout. This can

ABOVE: *The kitchen garden is not the only place for fruit trees such as this fruiting pear. Many fruit trees have exquisite blossom and colourful autumn foliage with the added bonus of a tasty edible crop. Planted in driveways, trained over arches, espaliered against walls or sheds or grwon for shade , the humble fruit tree has much going for it.*

LEFT: *Edna Walling philosophied on coming to terms with vegetable gardening. She deduced that the perfect means of enticement into this area of the garden, was to edge the beds with favourite plants and add colour, so that far from being a place of drudgery and hard work, it became a place of joy and productivity. In this backyard garden, lavender has been used to great effect as edging, roses provide much of the colour and fragrance, and the vegetables have been simply planted in with the flowers.*

ABOVE: *Rustic tin watering cans withstand the rigours of the weather far longer than their plastic counterparts. This vegetable garden is edged with old wooden cobbles set on edge and paths are spread with gravel laid over black plastic to arrest any weed invasion.*

LEFT: *A productive kitchen garden is tended in front of this country cottage. The custom of hiding the kitchen garden away from general view is not so widely practised today as gardeners recognise the visual attributes of an edible garden with its tapestry of greenery and texture.*

range from a simple 'no dig' plot in the backyard to a formal potager complete with espaliered fruit trees and hedges of berries and currants. Vegetables can also be grown successfully in the flower garden in true cottage garden style.

Traditionally, the kitchen garden was an integral part of every garden, providing the household with fresh fruit and vegetables for most of the year. Yet it was not for pure utilitarian purposes that kitchen gardens have become a custom; in many households, it is the domain of the male of the house, who, needing an outlet for his agrarian energies, can create an impressive culinary garden.

The custom of putting the kitchen garden away from general view is not so widely practised today as gardeners are recognising the visual attributes of fruit and vegetables. Their tapestry of greenery and texture can be as visually pleasing as many a flower garden, with the added bonus of supplying the family with fresh food.

'Out of sight, out of mind' is not a recipe for successful vegetable gardening. Far better to have the garden within sight of the kitchen window for the pure challenge of keeping it orderly as well as for the simple convenience of fresh produce for the table.

The art of successful fruit and vegetable gardening is an acquired skill with equal parts trial and error, elbow grease and sheer hard work. Soil, moisture, aspect and drainage aside, the critical factors are seasonal conditions and temperature requirements. While there are cool season and warm season vegetables, it is the length of the growing season that dictates where certain vegetables can be grown.

Ideally, the kitchen garden should be positioned in a northerly aspect in the Southern Hemisphere (a southerly aspect in the Northern Hemisphere) to receive as much sun as possible — at least four to five hours. Good drainage is vital with plots double dug and then built up with compost and mulch. Mulching is the key to high productivity.

The secret of tasty vegetables is to grow them quickly as flavour depends on the young growing tissue. The formula for a continuous supply of vegetables is small, successive sowings so that everything is not maturing at once. Ideally there should always be an empty bed ready for the next planting.

Organic gardening — working within the cycle of nature rather than controlling and destroying the soil with chemical fertilisers or toxic weedkillers and insecticides — is gaining greater appeal. The intent is to grow nutritious, tasty food in an ecologically balanced way. Compost is the key to growing strong healthy plants able to resist both pests and diseases.

Companion planting is another way of encouraging robust growth and it can also work as an effective pest repellent. Herbs such as parsley, thyme, borage, chervil, dill, sage and tarragon can be planted throughout the vegetable garden or used as garden edging. While it is widely known that garlic repels aphids, onions, rosemary and sage are useful for discouraging the carrot fly, and tomatoes deter the asparagus beetle. Lettuce, carrots and radishes are a successful combination and peas and beans promote growth in nearby plants.

Esther Deans, who pioneered the 'no dig'

vegetable garden method says that although gardens are not made by sitting in the shade and saying 'Oh how beautiful', they need not be made with hours of backbreaking toil. Her simple method requires no digging, negligible maintenance and has startling results. This unconventional type of garden, simply made using newspaper, lucerne hay, straw and compost, can be made on concrete, in old wheelbarrows or in elevated beds for ease of access for disabled gardeners in wheelchairs. Her book, *Esther Deans' Gardening Book — growing without digging*, is an inspirational source.

Kitchen garden designs can be as individual as any other form of garden plan and should not be too ambitious first time round. It can take many years to finally come to grips with the constant toil involved. The late Edna Walling writes in characteristic style on finally coming to terms with her own vegetable garden: 'I think I've got the hang of vegetable growing at last. Apparently you have to do a little messing around in the vegetable garden every day, or at least every other day.' This she achieved by planting some of her favourite plants in with the vegetables, to make the idea a little more appealing. 'I have started edging the paths with prostrate rosemary, hypericum and various thymes, and today I straightened my back and beheld a picture composed of the golden blooms of this hypericum and the quaint little white daisy-flowers of chamomile.'

If artistry is the means of enticement into the vegetable garden, a simple *potager* can be the answer. Evolved originally from the mediaeval monastery garden and then used widely by the

LEFT: *These vegetables have been grown the 'no dig' way with startling results. Layers of newspaper, lucerne hay, straw and compost have been laid directly on the cement, and are contained with wooden slabs. This unconventional but extremely effective way of growing vegetables has revolutionised gardening in inner-city areas where space is at a premium and for handicapped people who are unable to dig and bend as well as those gardeners who enjoy gardening without toil.*

French, a *potager* can be both ornamental and practical, combining vegetables, herbs and flowers in symmetrical patterns. It is wise to draw a pattern to scale before embarking on such a project as dimensions, proportions and symmetry are very much part of even the simplest design. Such a garden can be as simple as a square plot divided into four triangular beds totally enclosed by a path or hedge. Paths can add greatly to the charm of the garden and can look attractive made from old bricks laid in a herringbone pattern or from well-maintained gravel. The borders of each plot can be attractively edged with vegetables such as carrots or lettuce, herbs such as garlic chives, lemon balm or thyme, or flowers such as pot marigold, violets, nasturtiums or primroses. For a more formal look, lavender, rosemary or box hedging is effective.

The ultimate in kitchen garden design is the walled garden, but this is not conducive to all climates. In countries where there is a very limited growing period, the walled garden is an aid, particularly for espaliering fruit trees against, with the warmth of the walls encouraging fruit growth. In one well-known walled garden,

situated in one of Australia's less temperate areas, the heat from the walls was more conducive to 'stewing' the fruit than simply ripening. However, a walled effect can be created with wooden palings or simple hedges of berries. The pleasure of such a walled garden can be mitigated if the barrier is too high, effectively blocking much of the sunshine.

One of Australia's greatest examples is the Heide Kitchen Garden in Bulleen, Melbourne, originally created with great artistry some sixty years ago by Sunday Reed. Totally enclosed by a picket fence, festooned with roses such as Fantin Latour, *Spinosissima altaica*, Souvenir de la Malmaison and *Rosa Moyesii*, it includes some 300 herb, vegetable and flower species, and more than seventy species of roses. This national treasure has recently been restored, keeping its old world atmosphere intact, and is open for public appreciation.

Be it a simple vegetable garden or upmarket edible landscaping, the kitchen garden today is all the more enticing as we seek to not only make our gardens more productive but look for more palatable and healthy food alternatives.

The
NATURALIST'S
GARDEN

Touch this earth lightly.

AN ABORIGINAL ADAGE

While gardening has for centuries been the art of moulding the landscape into a pattern and taming plants from the wild to grow within, there is an essential part of us that still cries out for the inherent beauty of nature. Walks in the bush or woodland reveal touches of artistry rarely equalled by man. What we consider weeds in our urban environment have a beauty of their own when viewed in their natural territory.

To be close to nature is to have a simplistic vision of the environment, and to appreciate it is to marvel at such beauty. While the trend throughout the ages has been to use the garden as an art form — sculpting, colour co-ordinating and using foreign materials — there have always existed those that have quietly or passionately come to terms with nature, making their gardens sanctuaries for the common wild plants, grasses, birds, insects and animals. Here, native flora and fauna is encouraged to

ABOVE: *Early morning sun catches the intricate work of a spider's web.*

LEFT: *An ode to spring — a sea of golden daffodils carpeting the ground. A simple leaf-strewn path wends its way amongst the daffodils punctuated with rustic timber benches from which to stop and enjoy the scene.*

LEFT: *The intrinsic beauty of this garden rests to a large extent on the natural flow of water through the perimeter of the garden. Towering eucalypts grow along the river's edge, casting filmy reflections. Daffodils have been encouraged to naturalise in large drifts, embracing the onset of warmer weather.*

BELOW: *There is a gentle luminosity in this scene as the sun filters through, highlighting the crispness of the snow underfoot. The silhouettes of the bare trees add to the monochrome image with the soft blue sky providing the perfect complement of colour.*

RIGHT: *A scene of uncontrived beauty with the light filtering through to the leaf-strewn path flanked by helleborus.*

co-exist, weeds fade into insignificance and artificiality is deplored.

The simple joys of childhood are again appreciated — identifying a new bird call or type of butterfly or discovering a bird's nest woven so intricately from grasses, seed-heads and little twigs. Paths meander through the grass and under trees with no pristine lawns to continually call out for care. By filling the garden with native trees and shrubs, insects are more likely to abound, thus attracting insect-feeding birds. Water in the form of a pond, stream or simply a large clay bowl filled with water will also attract birds, whose presence adds a totally new dimension to a garden.

The subtle colours of moss-covered boulders, the simplicity of wildflowers and the unaffected beauty of the natural layout has its own appeal. While in Australia there is a growing appreciation for the eucalypts and wattles that so typify the Australian bush, in England the traditional flowering meadow is coming back into its own. There is much to be said for this renewed appreciation of our surrounding environment.

OLD-FASHIONED GARDENS

Show me your garden and I shall tell you what you are.

ALFRED AUSTIN, 1835–1913

There has been a welcome revival in both restoring and creating old-fashioned gardens. This rediscovery has also given us a renewed appreciation for the older varieties of plants with their enchanting names, their simplicity of form and heady fragrance.

The subtleness in form and colour of the old perennials have a charm that far outweigh their modern counterparts. The old varieties of columbine or granny's bonnet (*Aquilegia*) are grown as much for their unusual delicate-looking flower-heads as for their maidenhair-like foliage. Solomon's seal (*Polygonatum multiflorum major*), campion (*Lychnis*), tobacco plant (*Nicotiana sylvestris*), bleeding heart (*Dicentra spectabilis*), lamb's ears (*Stachys lanata*), statice (*Limonium*), paeony roses, delphiniums, hollyhocks, campanulas and madonna lilies are among the

ABOVE: *This single love-in-a-mist* (Nigella damascena) *is an old-fashioned variety not commonly seen.*

LEFT: *Irises are a traditional plant in many old gardens, planted here* en masse *for a wonderful spring display.*

old-fashioned favourites. The hardy old-fashioned biennial, honesty (*Lunaria annua*), grown for its mother of pearl seed-pods treasured by dried flower enthusiasts, self-sows easily and produces purple, white or pink flowers. A very old variety that pops up in our garden is a small-flowered purple-and-white-striped flowering plant. Similarly, the prolific self-seeder, love-in-a-mist (*Nigella damascena*), whose seed-pods are also sought after by dried flower arrangers, has the prettiest sky blue flower amongst feathery foliage, but in older gardens a single pale cream variety can be found. There are now pink and white varieties available commercially. The cheery, free-flowering red salvia (*Salvia grahamii*) sought after by children who drink the honey-like nectar, can also be found in very old gardens and old style nurseries.

Old roses are very much part of the old-fashioned garden and add a softness and ambience hard to create with modern plants. Roses have been a favourite with gardeners for centuries with their generous blooms, delicate hues and heady fragrance. The very names of many of the old-fashioned roses greatly enhance their charm: Chapeau du Napoleon, Jacobite Rose, Omar Khayyam and Souvenir de la Malmaison are among the few that evoke images of times gone past.

Among the bulbs, the old double daffodils are treasured for their uniqueness, while the tiny star-white bulb, star of Bethlehem (*Narcissus bulbodicum nivelas gillander*) can pop up in old garden beds along with the unattractive, but strikingly unusual dragon lily (*Dracunculus vulgaris*), which in full flight is almost as vulgar as the same suggests.

Shrubs such as Persian lilac (*Syringa persica*),the snowberry (*Symphoricarpus*), japonica (*Chaenomeles*), mock orange (*Philadelphus coronarius*), elderberry (*Sambucus*), winter honeysuckle (*Lonicera fragrantissima*), box (*Buxus sempervirens*), lavender (*Lavendula*), rosemary and the butterfly attracting buddleias formed the backbone of

ABOVE: *A shaft of late afternoon sunlight bathes this old-fashioned sundial in a soft light. Blue borage has self-seeded at the base.*

RIGHT: *Agapanthus line the drive in this historic garden, whilst aged olive trees filter the sunlight.*

many old gardens.

A garden brimming with old-fashioned plants conjures up nostalgia for the history and tradition of gardening. The charm, fragrance, colour and gaiety associated with such plants bring a feeling of lingering old-fashioned tranquillity into a garden. The names alone have a quaintness about them: granny's bonnet, lamb's ears, naked lady, sweet Alice, batchelor's button, mournful widow, bear's breech and kiss-me-quick are among the common names that have been handed down from generation to generation. It is said that the dear little forget-me-not, if planted on the grave of a loved one, would never die while the person who planted it lived. Such folklore simply adds to the enchantment.

The style of building can often dictate the type of garden design and planting scheme. A simple cottage is complemented by old-fashioned cottage plants whereas a grander home goes hand in hand with a more formal garden layout with hedging used to great effect, creating garden rooms. Box hedging is an old-fashioned favourite, and although keeping it trimmed neatly is time consuming it can add a pleasing touch of formality and antiquity.

Studying old garden photographs can stimulate design concepts and many nurseries now offer the rarer old-fashioned plant varieties, once again appreciated for their refined rarity and subtleness in form, fragrance and colour.

Garden features such as rose arbours, tile edging, hedges, paths, walls, simple fences, gates and follies or fancies were very much a part of

ABOVE: *A scented lily,* Lilium auratum, *rises out of the surrounding greenery, providing fragrance and elegance in this old garden.*

LEFT: *So often the style of home dictates the style of garden. The old-world design and planting in this garden complements the rustic architecture of the home.*

FOLLOWING PAGES: *An air of nostalgia pervades this rambling wild garden with simple white lawn daisies carpeting the lawn, like fallen cherry petals.*

the old style garden. Cactus, so often derided today, was an integral part of many old gardens. Rustic summer houses, conservatories, aviaries, bush houses or ferneries, however simple, usually sported fretted bargeboards and finials. Eccentric whimsies or follies played their role in the old-fashioned garden but a careful line must be drawn between careful artistry and nouveau garden 'kitsch'. Whereas enchanting rusticity can be the making of some gardens, tricksy new garden follies can ruin the whole effect.

A kitchen plot and orchard were included in most old style gardens. Deserted farmhouses, decades after habitation, still sport manifold varieties of fruit trees, still bearing prolifically despite their years of neglect. There is now a swing back to the old fruit and nut varieties,

which are unrivalled for pure taste. Compare the old gnarled mulberry trees, with their plentiful crop of large lush juicy berries, to the tasteless newer varieties.

Nostalgia for old world gardens is tied closely with our yearning for days long past. However, it is worth remembering, as you pour over faded sepia photographs of the gardens of yesteryear, that labour was often plentiful and inexpensive. You will get receive more satisfaction if you make your goal attainable. Whether restoring a period garden or creating an old style garden, keep to the tried and true perennials, shrubs and trees and away from the time consuming annuals and fussy little beds that constantly need attention. Once the garden is established it should then only need a gentle guiding hand.

GARDEN SEASONS

The SPRING GARDEN

*All nature seems at work. Slugs leave
their lair —
The bees are stirring — the birds
are on the wing —
And Winter slumbering in the open air, wears
on his smiling face a dream of Spring.*

SAMUEL TAYLOR COLERIDGE, 1772–1834

The promise of spring is fulfilled as swelling buds burst into bloom and the greyness of winter is replaced by an abundance of new growth. As memories of winter ebb, there is a distinct air of regeneration. Fragrances abound, hues are bright and cheerful and the garden becomes a haven for bird making nests and pollen-seeking bees.

There is untold delight in the first flower of spring — the herald of warmer days. As the garden awakens, there is renewed appreciation in attending the garden. In cooler climates where many plants lay dormant for months on end, each day in spring brings forth new

ABOVE: *The glorious hues of the oriental poppy* (Papaver orientale) *add brightness to a garden awakening from winter.*

LEFT: *Daffodils and prunus blossom herald the onset of warmer weather.*

ABOVE: *Drifts of daffodils provide a cheery welcome to spring and naturalise in most conditions, here looking perfectly at home amongst Australian eucalypts in a country driveway.*

LEFT: *The pale tones of* Tulipa saxatilis *are suited to the wilder perimeters of the garden.*

OPPOSITE: *A sea of* Chrysanthemum paludosum *carpet the beds of a vast sunken rose garden.*

delight. The brilliant hues of many spring flowering bulbs provide a cheerful awakening while subtler, less showy treasures have an enchantment of their own.

Deciduous trees burst into leaf or blossom, clothing bare limbs in a profusion of growth. The elm tree is one of the most ethereal in spring, with its delicate green blossom framed against the dark outline. Planted *en masse*, they are a wonderful sight. For the smaller garden, *Pyrus ussuriensis* (the Manchurian pear), is a handsome shapely shade tree with simple white spring blossom. Of the crab apples, *Malus spectabilis* and *M. ioensis* are among the most attractive in bloom. The stately tulip tree (*Liriodendron tulipfera*), has one of the most unusual subtle green flowers with prominent yellow stamens and is a most attractive shade tree. The dogwood (*Cornus*) family have a rare beauty of their own with a hundred or more species to choose from. *Cornus florida* is a slender small tree with large pink blossoms; *Cornus nuttallii* has stunning cream blossoms while *Cornus controversa* has more insignificant flowers. *Davidia* (the dove or

handkerchief tree) has a rare floral display with large, showy cream bracts lending a distinctive appearance. The magnolia family grow in a tremendous range of climates and produce spectacular fragrant flowers in spring, among the most most beautiful being *Magnolia denudata*, *Magnolia dempbellii*, *Magnolia kobus* and *Magnolia salicifolia*. Although not deciduous, many of the eucalypts have wonderfully fragrant gum blossom in spring, ranging from cream through to deep rose pink.

As John Brookes writes: 'The joy of seeing the first blossom unfurling from bursting buds is undiminished no matter how many times you have seen it before.' The fragrance of much of the spring blossom only serves to heighten the pleasure. Burying your nose into the boughs of a lilac bush or picking a handful of spring flowering bulbs is almost an elixir of youth. There is nothing like fragrance to bring back memories of youth. Perhaps children have a more imperceptible sense of smell or maybe they are more uninhibited in burying their faces into the very heart of a flower to draw the fragrance.

While many gardens are remembered for

their trees or architectural features, shrubs form much of the backbone of the garden. Used as hedging, ground cover, climbers, in a mixed border, in the shrubbery or as un understorey beneath large trees, their diversity is immense. Among the many attractive evergreens are *Rhaphiolepis indica* (Indian hawthorn); the dainty species camellias; the Australian native mint bushes *(Prostanthera* species); and the sweetly scented creamy-white *Daphne odora* 'Alba'. Deciduous spring flowering shrubs include the double mock orange (*Philadelphus* 'Virginal ' or '*Dame Blanche*'; *Magnolia salicifolia,* a large shrub with star-shaped white flowers and lemon-scented leaves; among the *viburnums, Plicatum var. tomentosum* or 'Mariesii' with their pure white flowers on horizontal branches; the elegant white-flowering *Stephanandra tanakae;* the unusual *Corylopsis glabrescens;* the pearl-bush (*Exochorda racemosa*); the lilacs; and the roses — climbers, shrubs, ground covers and standards in all colours and forms.

Grouping complementary plants together provides much of the fun and challenge in gardening. The pale green blossom of the Ukon cherry can look wonderful against the new blooms of the snowball bush (*Viburnum opulus* 'Sterile'), the snowdrop tree (*Halesia carolina*) underplanted with a mass of snowflake (*Leucojum vernum*) or snowdrop bulbs (*Galanthus nivalis*) provides a serene picture; while a drift of white forget-me-nots can look wonderful in a shrubbery amongst deutzias, philadelphus and white lilacs.

Bulbs provide a wonderful burst of colour with the brilliantly coloured tulips, cheerful daffodils and more elegant hues of fritillaria. Bulbs, more than any other plant, are most effective when planted *en masse* — in large drifts in lawns or under trees, or in groups in borders or beds. Some of the more unusual bulbs that add interest to the garden include the lily-flowered tulips (*Kaufmanniana hybrids* or *Tulipa viridiflora*); double daffodils (such as *Narcissus* 'Butter and Eggs', or Golden Ducat, White Lion, Van Sion, 'Telemoneus Plenus') or rare white hoop petticoat (*Narcissus bulbicodium*); deep wine coloured fritillarias; dainty scillas; and ornithogalums (*tenufolium* or *arabicum*). Hybridisation has resulted in larger, more colourful cultivars which are more suited to the structured areas of the garden, while the softer hues have great appeal in the wilder perimeters.

The
GARDEN
in
SUMMER

And the dew
Of summer nights collected still to make
The morning precious.

JOHN KEATS, 1795–1821

The heady days of summer may be enjoyed to the full within the garden. Vibrant sunshine, azure blue skies and bountiful growth are meant to be enjoyed in the great outdoors, enjoyment which is heightened by the abundance of blooms, riot of colour and heady fragrances which arouse the senses. Gardens are truly *en fête*, basking in their summer glory.

The garden takes on a mantle of greenery as the growing season is at its height. Garden beds come to the fore with perennials taking centre stage along with the lilies and daisies that are so much part of a summer garden. The dappled light provided by the upper canopy adds much to the allure of the summer garden.

ABOVE: *Canterbury bells* (Campanula medium).

LEFT: *Summer is a time for outdoor living and entertaining, when the garden is appreciated to its full extent. This blue-flowering* Salvia ulignosa *flowers throughout the summer months providing a hint of colour in an oasis of green.*

ABOVE: *Delphiniums are a magnificent summer flower, with their stately spires and generous blooms.*

LEFT: *The stately white spikes of* Acanthus mollis *(oyster plant) lend their support to the summer garden, planted here in front of a lavender walk leading to a brilliant flowering jacaranda tree in full bloom.*

OPPOSITE: *A perfectly sited swimming pool, this semi-oval, stone-paved pool is adroitly integrated into its surroundings. Using natural stone work to edge the pool and a spring-fed water supply, the pool seems to merge into the paddocks beyond. A ha-ha wall has been constructed on the bottom side of the pool, giving the impression that the pool provides the border between garden and countryside.*

In many areas of the world, summer goes hand in hand with incessant watering and in such areas, it is worth a total re-evaluation of planting and design. Lawns that need constant watering can be replaced with shaded areas of stone paving containing pockets of hardy alpines or herbs. A gravel forecourt shaded by a tree, such as the linden or lime (*Tilia cordata* or *petiolaris*); Chinese elm (*Ulmus parvifolia*) or the paper or canoe birch (*Betula papyrifera*), and scattered with terracotta pots would require little upkeep. I have seen aged wooden cobbles used most effectively on a large scale, lending a mellow provincial atmosphere.

Plant selection is critical. There are many plants that thrive on virtual neglect and need precious little water for sustenance. I was amazed one summer that, after four months without rain in southern New South Wales, in my garden the lavenders (particularly *Lavandula augustifolia*)

were a blaze of purple blooms, *Gaura lindheimeri* was a constant mass of delicate white blooms, the lilies put on a wonderful display, the old roses bloomed abundantly, the buddleias seemed to thrive on neglect and the *Erigeron*, thymes and daisies were as prolific as ever. It is too easy to become disheartened when treasures wilt and die and the whole garden seems to crackle underfoot. When your garden is at its driest, appraise it critically, seeking those plants that are not perturbed. Visit other gardens with a similar climate, or peruse nurseries for those plants that will survive. In dry climates, trees, once again, provide much needed shade from the direct sun, lending an air of restfulness.

I find green the most restful, cool colour in summer and am constantly amused, when photographing gardens, at the regret expressed that the garden was not at that time in full blaze. There is something immensely soothing about a

mantle of greenery, in all its many hues and textures. Shades of green are particularly effective where the use of too many conflicting colours can distract the eye and create dissonance as in small suburban or courtyard gardens. For all the colour within the garden, the redoubtable trees provide an important function of filtering sunshine and providing shade. The dappled light provided by the upper canopy adds much to the allure of the summer garden.

However, colour, when used with skill and artistry as Monet did at his famous garden, Giverny, is superb. There is much challenge in co-ordinating colours within the garden. As summer growth is rampant and flower life often fleeting,

it can become an exacting assignment to plan areas that will not only flower concurrently but be complementary in tone. Gertrude Jekyll used colours with much skill in her herbaceous borders, blending oranges, purples, yellows, blues, pinks and whites in with green and silver foliage to great effect.

A single colour theme also has great panache. A blue border can look stunning in the height of summer with the Tibetan poppy (*Meconopsis betonicifolia*), blue salvia (*Salvia uliginosa*), love-in-a-mist (*Nigella damascena*), delphiniums, larkspurs, hydrangeas and agapanthus in full bloom. These rich blues look good when highlighted by the dainty Queen Anne's

THE GARDEN IN SUMMER 93

RIGHT: *Wedding Day rose is smothered in small cream flowers in early summer, providing a haven for bees and a magnificent display for rose arbours such as this.*

OPPOSITE: *This cottage garden border is a mass of white-flowering plants, with the grey-leafed snow-in-summer* (Cerastium tomentosum) *backed by daisies, white poppies and the old-fashioned rugosa rose, Schneezwerg.*

lace or gypsophila, or the simple white or yellow daisies. Yellow provides a wonderful contrast to blue and the low growing, grey or green-leafed *Santolina* (cotton lavender), the bold sunflower, the yellow alyssum, helichrysums, golden marguerite (*Anthemis tinctoria*) or achillea are among the many yellow-flowering summer plants.

Warmer evenings encourage outdoor living and awareness of the garden may be heightened by planting some of the evening scented plants. There are actually a number of summer flowering plants that release quite heady aromas once the sun has set. The moonflower (*Calonyction aculeatum*) with its large white flowers unfolding at dusk, the evening primrose (*Oenothera biennis*) and night-scented stock (*Matthiola bicornis*) are among those plants which are best at dusk, while the lilies and pinks seem far more sweetly scented in the evening. Roses too are intrinsically linked with the summer garden and there are manifold species to chose from. The David Austin roses have understand-ably earned great popularity with their abundant blooms, delicate form and fresh fragrance.

Trees and shrubs can provide more than shade and greenery during summer, with some providing quite spectacular mid-summer blooms.

The jacaranda tree is a dazzling sight in early summer with its haze of mauve-blue blossom shown to great effect against the bare grey branches. *Magnolia grandiflora* is a massive tree with heavily scented cream flowers opening continuously during the warm weather. The Persian silk tree (*Albizzia julibrissin*) has a lavish display of unusual pink puffball flowers through-out the summer. The slender Lemon-scented myrtle (*Backhousia citriodora*) has sweetly scented leaves and clusters of cream flowers. Many of the eucalypt species flower prolifically during summer as do a number of Australian native shrubs, including grevilleas, hakeas, melaleucas and callistemons. As many plants indigenous to Australia are extremely hardy, they make for an easy care garden. They will also bring birds into the garden, which apart from their obvious appeal, their very presence will help protect the garden from pests. Among the many bird-attracting plants are Angophora, astroloma, banksia, calothamnus, correa, darwinia, epacris, kunzea, lambertia, leptospermum, lomatia, pittosporum, telopea and tristania. Those gar-dens on the fringes of the ever-expanding metro-polis or in the country, will also occasionally attract native fauna.

The GARDEN in AUTUMN

The place was a wilderness of autumn gold and purple and violet blue and flaming scarlet . . .

FRANCES HODGSON BURNETT,
The Secret Garden

The wonderful fiery days of autumn, when the garden is transformed into a tapestry of scarlet, crimson, maroon and translucent yellow, are one of the great bonuses of living in a cool climate. The garden undergoes a metamorphis with its mantle of greenery slowly turning leaf by leaf through delicate soft carmines to a fiery brilliance. This is a gentle time of enticement before the onset of winter.

Splashes of autumn brilliance breathe life into the garden at a time when there is little on show. A smattering of autumn tonings strategically placed throughout the garden will highlight certain areas, distracting the eye from those plants that simply shed their leaves without any

ABOVE: *Berry-bearing trees, such as this* Crataegus monogyna (*Common hawthorn*), *are a highlight of autumn.*

LEFT: *Autumn brings a mellow ambience to the garden — the sunlight is softer and the smattering of autumn tonings transforms the garden.*

glory. A cold climate is not the only prerequisite for autumn tonings. A deep rich fertile soil, preferably acidic, good air circulation and constant moisture (not to excess), along with a cycle of cold nights and warm days will bring out the pigments.

Some of the most brilliant displays come from the tupelo (*Nyssa sylvatica*), a large shapely tree which turns a brilliant red; the iron tree (*Parrotia persica*), which is shrub-like in appearance and colours a brilliant array of reds, yellows and maroon shadings; the smoketree (*Cotinus obovatus*), which unfolds from bronze through to clear red; the maidenhair tree (*Gingko biloba*), that most ancient of trees, which turns a pure clear yellow; the Chinese tallow (*Sapium sebiferum*); pistachio (*Pistacia chinensis*); the sargent cherry (*Prunus sargentii*) with its dazzling

red foliage; and the sweet gum (*Liquidamber styraciflua*) with its array of orange through to bronze foliage. Then there are the vast range of poplars, maples, plane trees, oaks, willows and dogwoods.

When the leaves carpet the ground, the sunlight is softer and thick dews carpet the garden in the mornings, there is renewed appreciation for the berry-bearing trees and shrubs that can be such a highlight of autumn. The *Pyracanthas* (firethorns), crab apples, viburnums, cotoneasters and rowans provide a wonderful range of coloured berries from white through to yellow and amber to the pinks, reds and scarlets. The spindle trees (*Euonymus sachalinensis*, *E. europaeus*, *E. oxyphyllus* or *E. yeodensis*) carry their vividly coloured berries along with brilliant autumn foliage. Many of the

old-fashioned roses have wonderfully bright coloured hips, such as the moyesii hybrids, most of the rugosa and spinosissima hybrids, eglant-erria, fedtschenkoana, virginiana, forrestiana, alba semi-plena, and the climbers, Wedding Day and brunonii.

Delicate autumn blooms can be provided by *Camellia sasanqua* with colours ranging from white through the many shades of pink to hot reds. These dainty flowers are quite strongly perfumed and can either be single, double or semi-double. As sasanquas love an acid soil and hate to be planted in any limed areas, sulphur can be sprinkled around the plants every few months to reduce the alkalinity. These dainty camellias are wonderful plants to espalier or to grow as a hedge, but also look charming in pots or as specimen plants within the garden.

Perennial autumn flowering plants include the delightful Japanese windflower (*Anemone hupensis*) which grows prolifically in filtered shade sending up tall stems of single or double white or pink flowers; the perennial aster (*Michaelmas Daisy*); the hardy yellow Golden Rod (*Solidago*); and the whole range of chrysanth-emums. Among the many bulbs flowering in autumn are zephyranthes, sternbergia, *Hedychium* (Ginger lily), and species of cyclamens, crocus, nerines, colchicum, liliums, galtonia and tritonia.

A number of Australian native plants flower during autumn, including the correas (native fuschia) with their colourful bell-shaped flowers so attractive to birds; the croweas with their masses of star-shaped flowers; *Grevillea triloba* and *Grevillea thelemanniana*; *Melaleuca lateritia*, commonly called the Robin Red Breast bush with

ABOVE: *Herbs can be picked and hung for drying in autumn, to ensure a supply for the kitchen during the winter months.*

RIGHT: *The contrast of these golden leaves against the lush evergreen backdrop, is one of the glories of autumn.*

OPPOSITE: *One of the great advantages of living in a cool climate is to experience the full beauty of autumn. To see the tapestry of colours and leaves carpeting the ground adds an enchantment to any garden scheme.*

its mass of bright red brushes; and the Queensland Firewheel Tree *(Stenocarpus sinuatus)* with its unusual fire red flowers.

Autumn is a tranquil time in the garden, a time for harvesting herbs and fruit and putting down some good compost from all the autumn leaves. I am at a loss to see how anyone could waste all those wonderful leaves by burning them. They make such wonderful mulch and compost down so rapidly. Even the most gigantic piles of leaves will break down to at least one-third volume within a few weeks. Either put straight onto the compost heap or put around the base of trees and shrubs and scattered over the emerging bulbs, they can only be beneficial.

While many welcome the cooler days for working in the garden, gardening writer, Mirabel

Osler writes of her personal autumn anguish: 'The onus, guilt and compulsion hang around my half-sleeping thoughts in the autumn days when the great bulk of summer has dropped over the horizon, when the clocks have changed and as a dormant animal, I'm looking for hibernation. Damn those fine mornings. It's then the guilt seeps in like a bad gas . . . I haven't the faintest idea what I should be doing out there. I don't want to know . . . The garden should be sighing and settling itself unaided into contented slumber.' Nature in fact needs little assistance in putting the garden to bed for the winter. Let the leaves provide their own protective canopy to the underlying plants and delight in the mellow days of autumn, all the more precious with the iminent onset of winter.

The WINTER GARDEN

Gardener, if you listen, listen well:
Plant for your winter pleasure, when the months
Dishearten; plant to find a fragile note
Touched from the brittle violin of frost.

VITA SACKVILLE-WEST, 1892–1962
The Garden

The appeal of the winter garden is subtle — the beauty of bare limbs, the delight of an unexpected fragrance and of the crisp clear air, and the pleasing snap of frost underfoot. Vistas are accentuated. Hedges come to the fore, creating garden rooms or providing lines of axis in the garden. Walls and paths form the skeleton and 'bones' of the garden whilst sculptural elements such as sundials and statuary take on a more prominent role.

Winter is a time for re-evaluation: How does your garden hold up without the abundance of summer blooms? Is the design structure strong enough to stand the test of winter austereness? It is a time of planning for

A B O V E :   *The unusual silvery-grey dried flower-heads of* Eryngium bourgatii *(sea holly) are part of the flower garden well into winter.*

L E F T :   *Proportions are pronounced and small details are hidden in a snowscape — evergreens come to the fore, stabilising the garden and providing substance and form.*

LEFT: *There is an element of magic following a snow fall — an overwhelming quietness and tranquility envelopes the garden and a sense of mystery is created especially when looking along paths and through shrubberies.*

OPPOSITE: *Silhouettes are enhanced by a light dusting of snow — the trees in this orchard take on a newfound beauty.*

the months ahead — making notes, sketching plans and delving into garden books. There is little of the frantic summer time watering, mowing and weeding.

A winter garden is the greatest challenge of all. I often ponder the idea of open days and garden competitions staged in winter to make both gardener and visitor more keenly aware of the unexpected beauty of a winter garden. Gardens with a strong element of architecture carry well through the winter months. The formal garden of stoned terraces and clipped hedges comes into its own. Alternatively, creating

a specific winter garden area in a secluded area of your garden can be particularly tantalising and rewarding. An enclosed area or courtyard can be selectively planted with fragrant winter flowering plants providing prositive inducement for enjoying the garden in the heart of winter. There is untold delight in finding the first bloom of the hardy winter treasures. I never fail to be stirred at the ephemereal beauty of the *Helleborus niger* with all its delicate looking, paper white flowers encrusted in frost or the subtle charm of the *Helleborus corsicus* blooming through a mantle of snow. The perversity of the plant world is

astonishing. One would expect any flower brave enough to flower through these months to be rigid and leathery. On the contrary, the delicate china blue *Iris unguicularis*; the sweetly scented *Chimonanthus praecox* or *Lonicera fragrantissima* ; and the unexpected blossom of the *Prunus mume*, with its fragrant pale flowers, are all ethereal in their beauty.

When the leaves carpet the ground and the garden beds lie unadorned, appreciation for the stalwarts of the garden, the evergreens, is renewed. Evergreens lend an air of permanence and dignity, examples of which are *Arbutus,* *Viburnum tinus*, acacias, berberis, camellias, *Clematis armandii, Choisya ternata*, eucalypts, daphnes,*Garrya elliptica*, hellebores, callistemons, iris,*Lonicera fragrantissima* or *L. nitida, Magnolia grandiflora* or *M. heptapetala*, pitto-sporum, pyracanthas, buxus, grevilleas, rosemary, bay tree and the ivies, grasses and ferns.

Immense pleasure can be gained from choosing plants suitable for the winter garden: seek shrubs with colourful berries or fragrant flowers, trees with interesting bark or silhouettes, early flowering bulbs and delicate hellebores.

Coming to terms with the garden in

ABOVE: *A strong element of architecture and design is pleasing during winter when the 'bones' of the garden are exposed. A walled garden provides shelter in harsh climates and is the perfect place for espaliering trees and shrubs.*

RIGHT: *A solitary* Mahonia aquifolium *flower at the base of this entrance pillar braves the first snow fall.*

OPPOSITE: *The crisp clarity of a blanket of snow accentuates a wide sweep of lawn.*

FOLLOWING PAGES: *Thoughtfully placed garden chairs are one of the most enticing forms of garden ornamentation, inviting reflection and beckoning reprieve from all manner of garden tasks.*

winter, particularly where winters are harsh, can take time. Rosemary Verey writes in *The Garden in Winter* how she came first to understand, then to appreciate the winter beauty. 'Many years ago, when I began to think about it, one thing puzzled me. Why did the countryside look so attractive and my garden so dead? It struck me then that a strange reversal takes place in the fortunes of countryside and garden from summer to winter. In summer our gardens are *en fête*, with their bright swathes of colour, while the countryside is demure in shades of green with the occasional pocket of wild flowers. I had to begin to appreciate winter scents, to notice the colour and tex-

ture of tree bark, to discover lichen and moss on the walls, to watch winter buds open and bulbs push their way through the soil. I began to realize that the structure of my garden is even more important in winter than in other seasons, because the bones become apparent and the eye is not distracted by beguiling planting. So the framework of my garden had to be set in winter.'

It is this acceptance of the subtle allure of the garden in winter that is an acquired pleasure. But perhaps greatest of all winter indulgences is garden dreaming. Sitting in front of a roaring fire making lists of summertime jobs and alterations without actually getting the fingernails dirty.

GARDEN FEATURES

SCULPTURE

One of the most compelling ways of commanding attention in the garden is with carefully selected and sited sculpture. Gardens are greatly enriched by even the simplest of statuary that may be remembered long after the garden fades from memory. Abstract or traditional, garden sculpture plays a vital role in garden appreciation.

The key lies in a restrained and critical appreciation of both choice and siting. Unless wishing to make a grand statement, simplicity and scale, together with form and texture are worth bearing in mind. As John Brookes warns: 'Most garden ornament is too grand by half and it immediately looks pretentious placed in a modest layout. Classic sculpture is for classic layouts unless of course you use it with humour. Far better is a humbler feature . . . associated with the correct plant grouping, or contrasted with wildness, this combination contains more charm on the scale of the average garden than a dozen temples or urns.'

Sculpture can either be used as a focal point, drawing the eye along a vista or path, or as a subtle adornment. The term 'planting sculpture' is not as absurd as it may seem. Much trial and error can go into choosing the appropriate site. One of the charms of using sculpture in the romantic or wild garden is the suprise element —

ABOVE: *The classic simplicity of a Grecian bust is an arresting choice of sculpture for a courtyard garden.*

LEFT: *The human form is the most arresting form of statuary, demanding attention and focusing the eye on a particular area of the garden. This classic sculpture has been perfectly placed at the junction of three long vistas, drawing the eye and inviting exploration.*

ABOVE: *This sculpture has been perfectly selected and sited, commanding attention yet looking at one with the overall design. Resting at the foot of a massive elm in a sea of forget-me-nots, the horses are a focal point but at the same time are in complete harmony with the garden.*

LEFT: *The moss growing at the base of this sculpture lends a feeling of antiquity and timelessness. Placed at the end of a long pergola in a small city garden, its very presence draws the eye to the bottom of the garden, inviting closer inspection.*

having the statuary rising out of a tangle of greenery or nestled into a private niche so that instead of commanding immediate attention there is great delight in its elusiveness.

Garden sculpture is presently undergoing a rebirth. While bird baths, sundials and garden pots have had constant appeal, sculpture and statuary are coming back into vogue. As with choosing furniture, the genuine antique will have that mellow patina and elegance that is hard to emulate in reproduction pieces. With statuary, an

original has enough presence to dominate any garden landscape. The danger lies in the mass market reproductions, which, despite their alluring price tag, tend to lose their appeal when the same piece is seen again and again.

Individuality in selection and siting of statuary is critical. A carefully placed sundial can attract interest to that section of the garden and can be formally placed on a marble pedestal or more informally, on a large boulder. Bird baths are perhaps the most practical form of garden

ABOVE: *The art of sculpture lies in individuality of selection and placement within the garden. The elegance of this urn is emphasised by its placement on a pedestal set against a plain background.*

RIGHT: *Bird baths are perhaps the most practical form of garden ornamentation. Anyone who has witnessed birds bathing will know the joy such a simple object can bring into a garden.*

ornamentation and these can be as simple as a terracotta saucer placed at the foot of a shrub or a washed out piece of driftwood under a dripping tap. Anyone who has witnessed birds bathing will know the joy such a simple object can bring into a garden.

Garden pots are a simple but very effective form of garden sculpture and can be as basic or elaborate as the budget can stretch. Terracotta is a marvellous medium, bleaching and streaking as it ages, giving it a warm, aged patina. Simple pots can be given an elegant touch with the planting of a standard bay tree, rose, box, camellia or honeysuckle. Conversely, grand pots can look stunning with the simplest planting or used as statuary and left purposefully empty.

The most peremptory garden sculpture is the human statue, which compels and commands attention. Sir George Sitwell's wonderful essay on gardens powerfully states they 'stir imagination, strengthen memory, banish the consciousness of self and all trivial and obsessive thoughts'.

Abstract sculpture is another sphere altogether and is far more personal. These are often used more for making a statement than providing harmony. Abstract statuary can best be offset by bold and unusual plant groupings that truly command attention. Few gardens can embrace more than one such work of art.

The garden, with its mass of greenery, provides the perfect background for displaying sculpture — the permanence of stone, metal or wood against the ever-changing vista of the garden.

WATER
in the
GARDEN

The mere suggestion of water in the garden is enough to give a touch of tranquillity and calm in even the most urban plot. A glint of water evokes a subtle sense of mystery while the added perception of running water adds another dimension.

There is perhaps nothing that can compete with natural water features: a simple stream running through the garden can be one of the greatest natural assets and gives the impression of space and breadth. On a far greater scale, those that look out on to the sea have an ever-changing vision splendid.

Throughout the ages water has been the quintessence of gardens. One only need look at the Persian, Moghul, Italian, French or Japanese gardens to know that water has been the very essence of their design. 'Fountains and waters are the soul of a garden', wrote Pierre Husson in his book *La Theorie et la Pratique du Jardinage* almost 300 years ago, 'How often it is that a garden, beautiful though it be, will seem sad and dreary and lacking in one of its most gracious features, if it has no water.'

A B O V E : *White arum lilies* (Zantedeschia aethiopica) *thrive in the moist conditions at the edge of this country lake.*

L E F T : *There is nothing that quite equals the charm of a simple lily pond in almost any size garden. In this garden, a backdrop of an old whitewashed brick wall overhung by a canopy of deciduous trees lends further enchantment.*

In a small garden, utilising water effectively and naturally can be an exacting task. The key to successful placement and use of water in a garden is making it the *raison d'être*. A water feature must be carefully implemented into the overall garden design so that the surrounding planting complements the feature.

Whereas formal pools and fountains have an elegance in their very formality, running water in the form of an artificial stream or pond must look uncontrived and natural to successfully integrate into the overall garden scheme. Most importantly, a pond needs to be in the lowest part of the garden, not at the top of a garden slope where it looks totally inappropriate. Pumps, however, can be utilised to rechannel water up the slope where it can tumble down over rocks and boulders as a waterfall.

While the sound of running water is refreshing to the spirit, there is something evocative in the stillness of a lily pond or a simple reflecting pool, and this is often far more attainable in the majority of gardens. Water is such a wonderful medium for reflection. Even

the look of fallen leaves on water has a spell of its own and the sparkle of water in a bird bath or simple wall spout gives that intangible extra something to a garden.

Waterside planting is most effective when kept simple. As the essence of water is coolness and tranquillity, an array of bright colours looks out of context. Most effect is gained from a mass of greenery and contrasting foliage with reflections from tree trunks and the changing moods of the sky. In the case of natural streams and rivers, sloping lawns dropping to the water's edge can be effective with bulbs planted in groupings at the base of trees. Waterlilies (*Nymphaea*) need calm and so are usually seen in the backwaters of creeks or in ponds. The white swathes of the arum lily (*Zantedeschia aethiopica*)

can look wonderful growing in a bold mass amongst reeds and rushes. The water buttercups (*Caltha palustris*) provide a splash of yellow against the mass of greenery and as one of the earliest spring flowering aquatic plants can be offset by daffodils growing on the nearby bank.

Whereas there is great delight to be had from watching birds bathe and play in water, there is a great responsibility as far as young children are concerned and this feature must never be overlooked. Ponds, however small and shallow, are enticing places for exploration which can so quickly turn into tragedy. In small gardens, raised pools offer some protection, however, the most effective childproof barrier is a fitted piece of sturdy wire mesh securely held just under the surface of the water.

GARDEN WALLS *and* HEDGES

There is no element in a garden that creates such a sense of privacy, or is such a tangible use of architecture, as a wall or hedge. They lend an air of permanence while providing the perfect background for foliage and offering a third dimension in planting.

By designing garden 'rooms', a sense of mystery is created. Even in the smallest area, walls or hedges conceal the entire garden, preventing it being seen in one glance. They direct the eye and can frame a view. On a more practical plane, they provide privacy, shade and shelter.

Hedges are one of the oldest forms of garden fencing, providing a 'living' garden partition. Evergreen or deciduous hedges at all different heights and in straight

ABOVE: *The beauty of a trimmed santolina hedge with its soft grey feathery foliage — here surrounding a bed of foxgloves, roses, iris and stachys. The slightly uneven look to the hedging has wonderful old world appeal and provides a much softer and more natural look than the traditional Buxus hedging.*

LEFT: *One of the most effective and fast growing forms of evergreen hedging is Lonicera nitida with its neat small leaves and vigorous growth. It withstands clipping well, making a dense compact hedge. A standard Buxus provides contrast with its larger leaves and balled head whilst the fragrant pink rose, Mme Gregoire Staechlin, on the rope swag above adds colour contrast.*

or curved lines can be used to create a sense of mystery, define space and add interest. A solid background of greenery is a marvellous foil for herbaceous borders, sculpture, furniture, gravel paths or simple lawn. Tall clipped hedges are obvious screening devices and can be grown from yew (*Taxus baccatta*), beech (*Fagus sylvatica*), blue Arizona cypress (*Cupressus glabra*), Irish juniper (*Juniperus communis hibernica*) or the wild olive (*Olea africana*). The English box (*Buxus sempervirens*) is one of the most widely used plants for low hedges, however, more informal unclipped hedges can be successfully planted with roses (Penelope, *Rugosa alba*, Iceberg, Celeste, Felicia, Frau Dagmar Hastrup), lavenders, santolina, rosemary, berberis, Mexican mock orange (*Choisya ternata*) or some of the Australian species such as the grevilleas, callistemons and leptospermums.

A romantic effect may be created using an existing hedge as the basis for a tapestry effect. Tapestry hedging is a more informal way of using hedges, and often provides year-round interest with flowers, berries, autumn foliage and an evergreen base in winter. An attractive combination is to use the *Viburnum tinus* as the base and intersperse it with an evergreen clematis and an evergreen summer flowering rose such as Wedding Day. The cream-white flowers would be almost luminous against the dark green background and would not require tedious clipping or pruning for a wonderful effect.

RIGHT: *This billowing cypress hedge is in fact shaped from a row of eight, century-old cypress bushes (Cupressus). The billowing shape is a feature of this historic garden whilst a path leads through an archway shaped into the hedge.*

OPPOSITE: *This dry stone wall is one of many used in rural areas to contain stock in countries throughout the world. The artistry and perseverance in building such expanses of walls is extraordinary and the fact that many have survived centuries of trampling by stock speaks volumes for their strength let alone their perennial appeal.*

Stone or brick walls are a more enduring and less time consuming form of partitioning within a garden although they need dexterous and capable hands to construct. They also need careful consideration in their placement and a sensitive eye in construction material. Stone walls with lashings of glaring grey cement can provide little beauty and similarly, spanking new brick walls have little of the charm of old brick walls that have weathered over the years and perhaps still have traces of their original whitewash.

Dry stone walling is perhaps the most natural type of garden wall, but it is an art that requires much toil, backache and artistry to perfect. Although an ancient craft, the skill may be perfected and considering the number of such ancient walls seen throughout the world, their durability speaks volumes for the builders' skill.

Traditionally dry stone walls are not bound with mortar, however, it is possible to achieve the same effect with the use of mortar in the core of the wall.

Ha-ha walls are a vastly under-rated way of blending garden into the surrounding landscape. A ha-ha is basically a sunken fence, invisible from above, but an impregnable barrier from below. Where the ground slopes away from the house, a ha-ha can be treated in almost the same way as a retaining wall, but on level ground, a trench needs to be dug with one sloping side and one vertical, usually supported by a stone wall. It is thought the ha-ha was originally spelt Ah! Ah! which was the exclamation of suprise on discovering, or falling over one! In country gardens they provide the perfect means for bringing the surrounding countryside into the

LEFT: Buxus *has been used to great effect for hedging in this garden with the lower variegated form providing contrast to the lush green lawn. The flowering crabapple* (Malus ioensis) *puts on a wonderful spring display.*

BELOW LEFT: *These dry stone walls are a work of art with their perfectly level top, stability and beauty of form. Walls have been used ingeniously in this garden to create 'garden rooms'. This wall divides an area of lawn from a walled 'wild garden' complete with forget-me-nots, daffodils and iris whilst the simple cherry plum providing spring blossom, shade, fruit and a sense of height to this very private garden.*

RIGHT: *A massive stone wall totally encloses this large country garden, lending a 'secret garden' appeal and creating a micro-climate within its walls. Blocking the worst of the winds and radiating warmth from the sun's rays, the wall also provides a wonderful backdrop and sense of form within the garden.*

garden while providing a stockproof barrier. In cities they can be used to full effect in harbourside or seaside gardens besides acting as a deterrent to stray animals.

The quintessence of garden walling is the walled garden, developed in classical times as an extension of the house. Medicinal and culinary herbs were grown in these micro-climates during the Middle Ages, developing into more refined horticultural showpieces during the Renaissance. Today they are rarely built, but a similar effect can be gained from tall hedging to create that wonderful sense of enclosure and to give that 'secret garden' feel. Improvisation can be used in the creation of such private areas by using existing structures such as tennis court or swimming pool fences covered in ivy or ramblers; or existing hedges linked together with simple trellis. A little licence has been used in our garden to give an effect of a walled garden. In an old orchard area, antiquated elms have suckered closely together to create two sides of the wall, another comes from an old fence now smothered in the evergreen winter flowering jasmine (*Jasminum mesnyi*) with the finishing wall coming from a tennis court fence covered with evergreen climbing roses (Silver Moon and Wedding Day).

Gertrude Jekyll writes at length on the charm of walls, giving many inspirational planting schemes such as moutan paeony and wreaths of *Clematis montana* on a low wall. 'I am for clothing the garden walls with all the prettiest things they can wear . . . I have a north wall eleven feet high, with a Geulder rose on each side of a doorway, and a *Clematis montana* that is trained on the top of the whole. The two flower at the same time, their growths mingling in friendly fashion while their unlikeness of habit make the companionship all the more interesting.' While walls are the perfect medium for covering with all your favourite climbers, some walls have greater impact if left quite unclothed, or at least with parts quite exposed.

The extensive stonework favoured by earlier designers has enabled many of their gardens to endure through the ages. Their art lay not only in the design, but in a subtle clothing of the walls. Abundant planting softens formality and gently clothes the architectural framework. A garden without framework is a transient thing, whereas garden walls can last centuries, providing an element of stability in a garden.

PERGOLAS

Pergolas are one of the most pleasing garden features for outdoor living or merely for adding another dimension to garden design. They have a myriad of applications: to provide a covered walkway, shelter an outdoor living area, frame a view or provide a welcoming front entrance. They may be free-standing or attached to the house and can be made from a wide range of materials.

Attached to the house, they act as an outdoor living room, filtering the strong sunlight and providing a subtle sense of semi-enclosure. In the garden, they lend a sense of permanence and formality, dappling a path with light shade so adding appeal and intrigue. A pergola entrance can make a delightful entrée into a garden or can transform a dull front patio or terrace.

To look out from the house onto inviting shady enclosures and fresh green foliage can add interest to even the simplest home. The concept of creating garden windows is not a new one but one that has great appeal in hot climates where to look out onto shady greenery is preferable to pulling the curtains.

Harmony in all garden construction is important, but it is mandatory in pergola construction. Material, scale and proportion are critical but vary with each construction. There is no right or wrong type of pergola, although

A B O V E : *Pergolas lend a sense of permanence and formality, and can effectively divide space within the garden.*

L E F T : *The classic beauty of this pergola rests on its generous dimensions and simplicity in planting. Wide enough to allow at least two people to walk along comfortably, the pergola has been constructed from massive drain pipes with timber overhead supports. In this large country garden, the pergola leads from the main garden area to the wilder garden on the perimeter.*

LEFT: *The simple construction is the key to this pergola's elegance. Constructed from large drainpipes with timber overheads, wisteria and Virginian creeper provide a shady walkway.*

OPPOSITE: *Although not a large area, this city garden has great appeal and has been cleverly designed to make the most of the available space. The statue at the end of this pergola draws the eye downwards and compels visitors to explore the lower part of the garden.*

certainly some constructions can look far more pleasing than others. It is said that there is no garden feature that is so misused. It is important to have a *reason d'être* — a destination or at the least a structure that provides transition from house to garden.

Edna Walling, the designer of some of Australia's most magnificent gardens, had very definite ideas on their design and construction. 'A matter that exercises the minds of some garden-makers is the breadth and height of pergolas, and to find oneself in possession of something meant to be a pergola that looks more like a monument to a daddy-long-legs is a little depressing! A low and broad effect is generally safer than anything tall and narrow. There can scarcely be any hard and fast rules about dimensions alike; so much depends upon the size of the garden, the position the pergola is to occupy, and the architecture of the house. But care must be taken to ensure that the scale and proportion of such features are right.'

Scale and proportion will vary according to the style and dimension of the garden, but as a general rule, a pergola should be wide enough to allow at least two to three people to walk through side by side. As a general rule of thumb, upright supports should be 2.4 m (7 ft) apart in length and width. If there is not room for this, a tree tunnel can be more appropriate. This is done by training trees or wisteria over a curved framework providing a less formal leafy walkway. A simple pear or quince allee can become the magnum opus of the garden and provide a relief from the traditional laburnum walk. As in all aspects of gardening, rare exotics do not always create the greatest effect. The most humble and unpretentious plants and structures can have the most stunning effect.

Rustic pergolas can be constructed from lightweight wooden poles with more permanent structures assembled from solid hardwood, brick, stone, metal, steel girders or rough cast cement. Overhead supports can be simple wooden battens

or bark-covered saplings. An important consideration is the aesthetics of the structure in the bare bones of winter. Bare gnarled wisteria or grape trunks have an eclectic appeal and can be complemented by judicious underplanting. A border of shade-loving plants (hellebores, wind anenomes, primroses, violets, Solomon's seal and forget-me-nots) can provide the transition between pergola and lawn or garden. Grass is difficult to establish in such shade, with paving or gravel a more suitable alternative.

Simplicity and consistency in planting has more visual effect than a 'bit of everything'. Alternatively, a single colour scheme utilising different types of plants can be striking. Wisteria (blue, white and pink fragrant racemes in spring) and ornamental or fruiting grape vines seem to give the greatest appearance of coolness. The delicacy of clematis (evergreen or deciduous), the fragrance of honeysuckle or jasmine, the brilliance of Virginia creeper in autumn or the old-worldly appeal of traditional rambling roses

provide alternative pergola coverings.

As I write this, I have spread before me myriad images of all types of pergolas for inspiration. So readily do they evoke such beautiful garden notions that my mind races with all types of possibilities. However, it is with a restrained eye that I look around my own garden and realise it is not just as simple as having a grand idea. Such structures can be among the most magnificent garden features, and many a garden will be remembered by their pergola alone. But they must look as though they belong to the garden as a whole, and to construct a pergola simply for the sake of 'having' one, can often be disastrous. This successful integration is one of the most challenging tasks in garden creation but well worth achieving.

Once clothed in climbing plants, a pergola adds to the feeling of mystery within the garden as well as adding a three dimensional feature that contrasts well with the fluid continuity of lawn and trees.

TOPIARY

Topiary has been used as a garden art form through-out the ages, swinging in and out of favour as trends varied. Scorned by some as too artificially contrived, it is embraced by others who welcome the formality and humour it can bring into a garden.

It has its forte in diminutive town or courtyard gardens where space is at a premium and the elegance of one or two pieces can provide the finishing touch. The classic pair of standard *Buxus*, bay or ficus at the front door is a timeless favourite. Individuality comes in place-ment and receptacles chosen. Classic pots and urns have great appeal, as do weathered terracotta pots.

On a larger scale, whole trees or hedges have been cut into fantastic shapes and these have become the *pièce de résistance* in a number of select gardens. In some instances, topiary is included within the garden simply for the fun of it and should be appreciated for its quirkiness rather than any ponderous sensibility.

Topiarists must have infinite patience and dexterity with clippers and shears and be prepared to keep the plants in the peak of health with regular watering and generous fertilising. It can also take much trial and error working out premium times to trim. Pruning or clipping

ABOVE: *A train shape has been fashioned from the small-leafed* Lonicera nitida *in this terracotta windowbox.*

LEFT: *Evergreen privet* (Ligustrum vulgare) *is well suited to the art of topiary. These privet hedges, with their simple geometric shapes, create a pleasing sense of order and provide a dramatic focus in the garden.*

should taper off towards the end of the growing season so there is an even cover of greenery throughout the winter months.

Plants suited to this type of art form include *Buxus*, bay, cypress, fig, cotoneaster, yew, ivy, abelia, camellia, westringia, honeysuckle margeurite daisy, oleander, rose and grevillea. In fact any evergreen small-leafed plant is suitable and much fun can be had in experimentation. The standard shape of the balled head is the easiest shape to master. To try this simple shape, take cuttings from the required plant, choosing a straight single stem as the base. It is often helpful to tie the stem to a stake to keep it straight. Side

RIGHT : *Whilst buxus, privet and bay trees are the most commonly used topiary plants, any evergreen shrub can be utilised, as illustrated by this three-tiered holly bush.*

BELOW : *The English box* (Buxus sempervirens) *is one of the most popular choices for topiary because its shiny dark green leaves provide a dense growth of greenery perfect for ornamental training. When placed in large matching terracotta pots they add touches of elegance and formality to any garden design.*

OPPOSITE : *Weeping figs* (Ficus hillii) *trained as standards are used to enhance and complement the entrance way to this contemporary -styled building.*

shoots should be rubbed off as they appear and as the head forms, lightly clip the new growth into shape. For more intricate shapes, branches can be wired into position or wire frames used to train the plant on to. Interest can be added by having two or more plants growing together with their stems twisted or plaited. There is no limit to the shapes: animal forms, chess pieces, spirals, or wreaths are only some of the possibilities.

The decorative form of topiary can be all that is needed to create a focus within a garden. It also provides a contrast to the classic lines of period gardens, offsets a natural style garden or provides a sense of whimsy in a formal garden.

GARDEN GATES

The power of suggestion is a subtle yet effective way of providing added interest in garden design. To lure the visitor from one garden scene to another by inviting rather than revealing all is the secret to many of the most interesting gardens. Leaving a garden gate ajar is a compelling invitation for further exploration by enclosing and yet partly revealing the garden beyond.

The type of garden gate can greatly add to the atmosphere and ambience of a garden. Possibilities are infinite — in a simple garden, a garden gate can provide a touch of elegance or rusticity depending on the style of garden. They can be a feature of a garden or blend in harmoniously without causing impact.

Entrance gates can create anticipation of the garden within and often reflect the garden style. Whereas a simple wooden picket gate often symbolises a cottage type garden, the elegance of wrought iron reflects a more formal style. Some of the most compelling entrances are those that are constructed as a barrier without impeding the view or those that are complemented by careful planting.

Gates can be designed for privacy, security, to keep children in and animals out or for pure aesthetics. In keeping with the rest of the garden, the garden gate

ABOVE: *A gate at the end of a path lures one on and adds interest to the overall garden design.*

LEFT: *Gates left ajar issue a compelling invitation for further exploration by enclosing and yet partly revealing the garden beyond.*

ABOVE TOP: *A classic white-painted picket fence and gate enhance and complement the cottage-style garden and house framed within.*

ABOVE: *A typical early twentieth century woven wire and wrought iron 'Kangaroo' single-hand gate, seen in many old cottage and farm gardens and presently receiving renewed appreciation.*

LEFT: *This hand-crafted tea tree gate is perfect in its simplicity, adding much to the ambience of the garden.*

should complement the fence flanking it. Timber gates are more suited to timber fences, simple wire gates are suited to country or cottage gardens and wrought ironwork for town gardens.

Enclosing an area of the garden with hedges or walls can be the perfect excuse for a gate. A gate allows some of the garden beyond to be glimpsed and invites exploration of such an area. This enclosure can be particularly effective in the overall garden design, lending an air of formality and permanence. Such an enclosure can simply be a herb or kitchen garden; a formal area of lawn and pool; a children's play area; a private outside entertaining area with flagstones and shade trees; or a simple lawn area with a comfortable chair sheltered under a leafy canopy.

ABOVE: *Pickets are a traditional form of fencing — creating an effective barrier yet allowing for some visibility. The styles of picket fencing are numerous — from rough-hewn split timber to the more traditional dressed timber palings with carved tops. In this established garden, elaborately turned finials on the gate and corner posts create a distinctive front entrance for the elaborate Victorian gate.*

RIGHT: *Garden entrances greatly reflect the type of garden within — these elegant gates mark the entry into magnificently landscaped grounds beyond.*

Down the GARDEN PATH

Paths are among the most important of garden elements, providing an important function as well as drawing the eye onwards. They not only encourage exploration but are the service area for feet and wheelbarrow. Enhancing and complementing the garden, paths not only decree where we walk, but from what angle we view the garden.

They also, to a certain degree, reflect or dictate the type of garden style. Winding gravel paths seem to go hand in hand with a cottage style garden while grass walkways are for a more formal effect; dressed stone or slate paths give an ordered feel to a garden while cutting a swathe in long grass gives the suggestion of a pathway in a wild garden.

Garden writers through the ages have had their different views on the garden path: J. C. Loudon believed paths need not lead anywhere in particular while Russell Page resolutely believed that a path must lead somewhere. Richard Sudell wrote that paths make a garden while Hugh Johnson says a garden should have as few paths as

---

A B O V E : *Simple rectangular paving stones set into gravel add a touch of elegance to this garden scene. The ornate Victorian aviary provides a focal point.*

L E F T : *Winding brick paths are perfectly suited for the romantic garden or wilder sections of the garden. In this case, the bricks have been laid in a simple stretcher bond pattern and by allowing the bulbs and grass to naturalise between the bricks, the pathway does not become too much of a feature, but rather blends into the surrounding greenery.*

possible: 'Too many look, and make the looker feel, indecisive.'

With all this conflicting advice, it seems wise to take the matter into your own capable hands and let your head dictate the type of path. The garden style largely dictates whether a path be intimate or wide in breadth, straight or winding, of paving, brick, grass or gravel. The one true requisite is suitable drainage. As they are the service area of the garden, they must not be sodden and waterlogged.

Gravel paths have a natural look about them and can be greatly revitalised by raking for an instant facelift. The odd weed can be chopped, sprayed or doused with boiling water. Brick lends itself to a variety of patterns and quickly assumes an old world character. Old bricks or 'seconds' have greater appeal than perfect new

ABOVE: *Large concrete pavers provide the touch of formality needed for this long walkway, which is flanked on both sides by helleborus.*

RIGHT: *Grass walkways are one of the most restful forms of pathways, although perhaps necessitating slightly higher maintenance than stone, brick or gravel paths. The green of the walkway complements the foliage in the flower borders flanking the path.*

OPPOSITE: *Old terracotta edging tiles give a more finished edge to this gravel walkway.*

specimens and can be laid in basketweave or many forms of herringbone patterns. Long lines running along a path can emphasise its length while lines running across give a feeling of width.

Simple flagstones or sawn logs set in lawn can be as informal or elegant as the garden dictates. When laying such a path, the simplest method of placing the flagstones is to walk naturally along the lawn, placing a piece of stone at each footfall (60–70 cm, 24–28 inches). The surface of the stepping stone should not protrude above the lawn as the mower should be able to run over the area without making contact. As with all paths, it is important to actually have a reason for its existence, a purpose other than for pure aesthetics. One of the most restful pathways is a simple grass walk, although this is impracticable in a well-used traffic area. Crazy

LEFT: *Paths need to be in keeping with the surrounding garden. This informal gravel path strewn with fallen spring blossom is in tune with the nostalgic garden atmosphere that pervades this garden.*

OPPOSITE: *Large, irregular, paving stones have been set with great precision in a gently curved path to the front entrance of this large city home.*

paving can be, as the name suggests, crazy. Unless sympathetically done, implementing natural coloured stone and bonded with similar coloured cement and perhaps softened by low growing plants such as thyme or arenaria, the effect can be too contrived.

Cobblestones, pavers and cement blocks will provide a hardwearing durable surface and are available in a range of colours, textures, sizes and interlocking shapes. Preparation is vital in the construction of paving, and actually takes more time than the laying of the pavers.

In the native garden, a simple dirt path or litter of woodchip complements the natural planting style and blends in harmoniously. To soften any pathway, soft planting on both sides of the path will give a more natural effect than a path placed smack against a house or fence. The scale of the garden and home will also greatly dictate the dimension of pathways. As a general rule, paths should be wide enough to walk two abreast (1 m; 3 ft), although an intimate winding path leading through the shrubbery is just as appropriate as a wide grass walkway dividing the herbaceous borders.

Continuity within a garden is another important consideration and a more pleasing picture can be composed of all stonework, or all brickwork, rather than a jumble of concrete, pavers and gravel paths. Perhaps more than any other garden feature, simplicity is the key for successful garden paths.

The
GARDEN
CHAIR

As gardens are for solace of body and soul, so the garden chair is the place to sit back and enjoy it from. How inviting and alluring they can be, nestled in the dappled shade of a large tree on a warm summer's day, or catching the last shafts of sunlight on a winter's afternoon. An inviting seat from which to stop and contemplate the garden can provide the fundamental touch in any garden.

It is important that garden seating look permanent and good placing is vital. It is worth lugging around for some time until a suitable locale is chosen — as a focal point at the end of a vista, strategically placed amongst a clump of trees or nestled into a specially made arbour. Placed thoughtfully, they invite reflection and lure you to sit and enjoy the fruits of your (or other's) labours. I often wonder how many garden seats are really sat upon by their owners and how few gardeners really sit back and bask in their garden's glory. They may sit and dream, but it is usually of future schemes requiring hard toil.

I have heard it said that a garden without a seat is not a garden, not unlike a theatre without a stage. However, many garden seats are chosen for purely aesthetic reasons rather than their utilitarian use. Some of

---

A B O V E : *This rare Bentwood two-seater is sheltered from the elements on the verandah of an old country home.*

L E F T : *Placement of garden seating is paramount as illustrated by the appeal of this teak bench nestled under a grove of elms.*

LEFT: *A secluded and peaceful retreat from the elements — sheltered by the leafy roof of a tree canopy, these chairs provide a shady haven for spectators or players from the adjacent tennis court.*

the most appealing-looking seats can be hellish to sit on. Stone seats, while looking elegant and inviting, are decidedly cold and uncomfortable. And while nothing can surpass the elegance of wrought ironwork, as delicate and attractive as it may appear, it can be most uncomfortable. Rustic furniture made from irregular boughs of wood dowelled together can offset many a garden but again is meant more for ornamentation.

Wood deservedly earns its place as the most popular and versatile medium and is the most comfortable to sit on. Hardwoods like teak are not only weather resistant, but require little maintenance, last indefinitely and weather to an attractive silver-grey finish which complements

any garden scheme. Softwoods such as pine are a more economical proposition and can be treated successfully with timber preservatives to extend their life. There is no end to the variety of designs to be made from wood — from the formal English Lutyens bench seat to the simple weathered log slung between two mossy boulders.

Wooden furniture, if left unpainted, blends into the garden scene with more sensitivity than the glare of new paint. Gertrude Jekyll writes of white-painted furniture as 'deplorable', focusing too much attention onto the object rather than the garden. She suggests this may be mitigated, by adding a good deal of black and raw umber to the white, 'till the paint is of the quiet

FAR RIGHT: *A rare early Australian chair known as a 'Cootamundra Jack' has been handcrafted from unusually shaped tree limbs and even wooden sewing spools!*

RIGHT: *The deep green of this attractive cane garden setting is in perfect harmony with the surrounding garden — its simple elegance of form offsets the expanse of lawn. Nestled under a leafy canopy, the natural grouping has a welcoming air that invites use.*

BELOW RIGHT: *Painted cane furniture has perennial appeal — the paint protects the furniture from the worst of the elements and provides a certain uniformity where different styles are grouped together.*

RIGHT: *A traditional two-seater teak bench, set against a background of ivy and climbing roses. The natural lustre of the wood has more appeal than layers of paint that need constant upkeep.*

BELOW: *Wood deservedly earns its place as the most popular and versatile medium for garden furniture — it is hardy enough to withstand the elements and comfortable to sit on.*

OPPOSITE: *This quaint bush timber seat has great individuality and charm in its cottage garden setting.*

warm grey that for some strange reason is known to house-painters as Portland-stone colour'. The fashion that has thankfully shifted from white paint to National Trust green (deep bottle green), can also be improved on by choosing a more subtle, matt, pale grey-green. Garden seats need not necessarily be constructed as such. Some of the most informal garden seating arrangements can be as simple as a low 'sitting wall', broad and low enough to invite repose; a boulder; or for more complete relaxation, a hammock swung between two shady trees in a secluded corner of the garden.

The garden is such a perfect setting for entertaining or family living, that even collapsible canvas or light wooden chairs which can later be protected from the weather under the shelter of a verandah or stacked in a garage (carport) can be indispensable. The garden is said to inspire free-thinking — after all, wasn't Newton seated under an apple tree when he conceived his gravity principle?

TABLES

Outdoor tables effectively turn the garden into an external living area and for this reason alone their inclusion as part of the overall garden scheme is indispensable. As their sheer size usually precludes them from much mobility, they need to be weather resistant, sturdy enough not to overbalance at the slightest touch, not too glaringly obvious, and yet functional.

If space is limited, for example in a small courtyard garden, portable or fold-up tables with brightly coloured throwover cloths, can be an alternative. Trestle tables can be stored neatly in a garage (carport) and set out on the terrace or under the shade of a tree when needed.

When selecting outdoor furniture, it is worth remembering that a permanent fixture is more likely to entice you outdoors at meal time than a table that needs assembling and dismounting at each use.

Weathered or painted cast iron tables can be topped with teak, sandstone or marble slabs. Softwoods, such as pine, are light to move, but need annual timber preservative treatment to keep them from deteriorating while hardwoods, such as teak, need little maintenance and weather well. Hand-forged iron can lend a whimsical air while hand-crafted bush furniture gives a look of individuality.

ABOVE: *Outdoor tables effectively turn the garden into an external living area, and as such they need to be able to withstand the elements, be functional and sturdy enough not to overbalance. Rather than take centre stage and be too glaringly obvious, outdoor furniture needs to blend in with the garden background, as does the black-painted setting in this courtyard garden*

LEFT: *The intimacy of this setting under a leafy pergola is enticing enough to use throughout the warm summer months. Painted green, the table and chairs blend in with the canopy of grape and roses.*

ABOVE TOP:
*Verandahs provide the ideal
outdoor living area for
entertaining and family living.
These smartly painted director's
chairs provide great versatility as
they may be easily moved out
into the garden or folded away.*

ABOVE: *The elegance and
durability of wrought iron make
it a favoured option for
permanent outdoor furniture. It
also has a timelessness that adds
elegance to any garden scene.*

LEFT: *Marble is perhaps
the most durable of all table
surfaces, and in this garden, set
atop a wrought iron base, the
marble blends in with the*
Clematis montana *draped
above and the* Erigeron
growing at its feet.

Topped with cotton tablecloth, oil cloth or baskets of flowers; sheltered by a large umbrella, pergola or tree canopy; flanked by solid wooden benches or elegant iron chairs; or simply accentuated by the style of planting in the garden, tables make an attractive and practical addition to any garden.

Leafy pergolas or shady verandahs provide the ideal outdoor eating and entertaining areas, providing relief from the direct sunlight and yet offering enticing views of the garden. A distant view of the harbour, secluded garden or leafy courtyard holds greater allure than the actual table structure.

ABOVE: *Old sewing machine bases are much sought after as bases for outdoor tables as they provide an individual base for a marble slab.*

TENNIS COURTS

Where space allows, tennis courts provide one of the most wonderful forms of home entertainment. There are, however, two schools of thought on the placement of tennis courts within the garden. Non-tennis players firmly believe a tennis court should be hidden from view, while families that enjoy tennis and use the court regularly believe the court should be as close to the house as possible so that the tennis may be viewed from the shade of verandah or terrace. As anyone who plays tennis knows, much entertainment can be had in watching a good game in progress, so wherever the placement, it is wise not to screen the court entirely from view.

With the range of materials available for surfacing and fencing, it is possible to design a court in sympathy with the surrounding garden. A grass court with catch corners instead of an entire fence can be one of the most aesthetically pleasing courts in a small garden. The grass court area can also double as an outdoor entertaining area or children's play area. One of the most wonderful tennis courts I have seen is a sunken grass court with no unsightly barriers to keep the balls in — they simply roll back down the slope onto the court.

A B O V E : *A tennis roller stands sentinel at the entrance to this grass tennis court — grass courts are perhaps the most aesthetically pleasing surfaces within a garden because they blend in with their surrounds more naturally.*

L E F T : *An old-fashioned tennis roller provides a touch of whimsy to this country tennis court.*

LEFT : *Designing a court in sympathy with the surrounding garden is not always simple, but by allowing climbers such as* Clematis *and rambling roses to soften the metres of wire fencing, an unsightly barrier is eliminated.*

BELOW : *This tennis pavilion has the added bonus of looking not only to the tennis court, but outwards along the verdant green walkway to a Spanish urn flanked by lush herbaceous beds.*

The actual playing area of a tennis court requires a great deal of space, but it is equally important to surround the playing area with a generous space. There is nothing more frustrating than being thwarted by the back fence in your attempt to return the ball. A good overall playing area needs to be at least 33 m by 14 m (36 yards by 15 yards).

A level surface is needed for the court and this can then be surfaced with grass, clay, asphalt or one of the newer all-weather surfaces that need no rolling or marking and repel moisture. The tennis surround can be netting with timber or iron supports or for a more individual look trellis can be used to great effect.

In one of the rare mentions of tennis courts in the myriad of books on garden design, Richard Suddell gives an example of using trellis. 'Here is a treatment which creates beauty without detracting from the utility of the surround. Roses

are trained to a very wide-meshed trellis,
designed to give a window effect. This does not
hide the tennis court, but takes away the
appearance of bareness produced by the netting
and its supports.' An evergreen surround, he
believes, is another way of softening the boundary. 'The surround to a tennis court is a feature
that can make or mar a garden design', he writes.
'Nothing is more unsightly than a vision of rusty
iron supports and tall stop netting.'

Tennis pavilions or simple shelters to sit
and view the tennis from require much thought
in design. They need to be large enough to seat
at least half a dozen people and have adequate
storage room for keeping the net, marker and
extra fold-up chairs. A simple rose or clematis
covered structure can complement a rambling
country or cottage garden while a smart
architect-designed pavilion can add to the
elegance of a more formal garden and home.

LAWNS

T here is no one garden task that gives such an instant lift to a garden as that of mowing the lawn. Even the most neglected garden can be given an immediate facelift. However, lawns are not all they seem. A garden of 'lawns and trees' conjures up a restful scene and is usually put forward as the ideal low maintenance garden by those that despise flowers. However, beware — they require pampering, patience and penance.

Not unlike keeping a pet, lawns require regular feeding, watering, trimming and much tender loving care. They not only need tremendous preparation to become established, they then require constant maintenance. In many climates weekly mowing is necessary, but even this is not as simplistic as it sounds. A mower of some sort is needed — these need careful and constant care for fear of becoming temperamental. Sit-on mowers are a wonderful way to cover large areas but they do not always manoeuvre well under trees and awkward corners. Push mowers are a more unrelenting way to come to terms with the garden but are not always a successful tool in inexperienced hands. There are few who have not experienced the pique of finding their star bulbs mown down or a precious shrub mown over. Whipper-snippers are another dangerous tool in the hands of anyone but the gardener — trees and shrubs are easily ringbarked — but are a wonderful way of doing the edges.

ABOVE: *Herbal lawns are a romantic alternative in areas of little traffic. The tiny white-flowering carpeting thyme is* Thymus serpyllum minimus, *while the larger purple-flowering variety is* Thymus vulgaris.

LEFT: *This enclosed lawn area has added interest from the bird bath and surrounding sculpture.*

LEFT: *A feeling of intimacy is experienced on entering this small enclosed lawn through the hedge of rosemary* (Rosmarinus officinalis). *The use of space is a paramount element in garden design and lawn is one of the most effective means of implementation.*

OPPOSITE: *Flowering ixias merge into the lawn beyond, softening the outline.*

'The edges' are another matter altogether. When it takes hours to mow the lawn, there can be precious time left for handcutting the edges. Edging garden beds with plants that can be mown into can be quite successful. Such plants include catmint (*Nepeta*), thyme (*Thymus vulgaris* or *carnosus*), alyssum (*Lobularia maritima*), babies' tears (*Erigeron mucronatus*), bugle flower (*Ajuga reptans*), snow-in-summer (*Cerastium melaleuca*), pennyroyal (*Mentha pulegium*), or the simple lawn daisy (*Bellis perennis*).

Much has been said for and against lawns by designers, gardeners and writers. English garden writer, Mirabel Osler, equates making lawns with washing up: 'Why do experts go on so about lawns?. . . What is the spell and fascination of spending such a disproportionate amount of time on this one gardening subject when so many others have more allure?'

Away from the tyranny of such manicure-dness, an artistic effect can be created by the natural use of grass. In a larger garden, cutting

swathes through areas of long grass or mowing areas of lawn at different heights can lend a beguiling air to the garden. Areas of lawn naturally planted with bulbs can be left unmown for months while the bulbs 're-energise', creating quite an artistic effect in out-of-the-way areas.

Lawns are designed to give space and depth to a garden and act as a foil to the colour and texture of the shrubberies and beds. Open space is paramount to good garden design. They are also wonderful play areas for children's ball games or garden picnics. I am probably not the only one who has made the mistake in their very first garden of ruining what could have been a wonderful open lawn area by dotting trees around. This is planting for planting's sake rather than with any eye for design. Open sweeps of lawn can be far more visually attractive than such a hotchpotch of specimens.

Low demand landscapes, economising our natural resources as well as our own labour reserves, are now being considered as the sensible alternative to the needlessly fussy, high resource and maintenance gardens. The 'perfect' lawn is the greatest consumer of energy — not only human but also in the form of fertilisers, weedkillers and water. The concept of the natural flowering meadow is coming once again into its own. Using native grasses, mowing need only be done once a year in autumn after seed has been set, leaving a grassy cover. This type of natural lawn can be complemented by a mixture of wildflowers, herbs or simple self-seeding exotics.

Ground covers offer another alternative to lawns, and once established, require almost nil maintenance. In areas of dense shade, it is often easier to underplant with suitable alternatives so that the soil is covered with mat-forming ivies, hypericums and periwinkles. Herbal lawns are a romantic alternative in areas of little traffic.

Chamomile (the non-flowering variety, 'Treneague') is quite hardy once established and is easily propogated by division or cuttings taken in spring. Prostrate thyme (*Thymus serpyllum*) or the woolly thyme (*Thymus lanuginosis*) will grow in gravelly soil and once established as a lawn, can be mown with blades set high.

Much has been made of herbal lawns since Vita Sackville-West wrote of her experiment with a thyme lawn: 'I decided I must have something very low-growing, which would not suffer from the wind . . . and dibbled in lots and lots of the common thyme, and now have a sort of lawn which, while it is densely flowering in purple and red, looks like a Persian carpet laid flat on the ground out of doors. The bees think that I have laid it for their especial benefit. It really is a lovely sight; I do not want to boast, but I cannot help being pleased with it; it is so seldom that one's experiments in gardening are wholly successful.'

The choice of lawn depends largely on the style of garden and home. The subtle greys and olive greens of Australian plants call for mossy rocks, native grasses, fallen bark and ground cover plants in the place of lawns while small town gardens often utilise large areas of paving, softened by greenery, negating the need for lawns. Country gardens depend largely on sweeping lawns to give breadth and interest to their gardens, which are usually on a far larger scale than allowed in suburbia. In Australia, these lawns also serve effectively as bushfire breaks, often saving homes from burning, as well as providing a veritable oasis in an often drought stricken environment.

As in all manner of gardening, lawn preferences must equate with personal lifestyles. As some have the time and inclination to have spotless homes and gardens so do others gain great pleasure from a more woolly romantic look.

WINDOW-BOXES

Windowboxes are one of the few places where an absolute riot of colour can be used to stunning effect. In fact it is almost a maxim for windowbox planting that the brighter and more varied the colours the better. They can brighten up a dreary outlook, frame a view or distract from a bad one. They can also provide a cheerful first impression and, in many units, they serve as the total garden. Certainly my first impression of London, training in from Heathrow Airport, was of gaiety and colour with a lively array of windowboxes brightening the late winter gloom.

Unfortunately many window ledges are not built wide enough to accommodate a windowbox, but where they are, they should be utilised to the full. A riot of herbs on a kitchen sill can provide not only freshly picked herbs, but fragrance, beauty and colour.

Special planter boxes can be built from hardwood with holes drilled in the bottom for drainage or, for a continual display of colour, individual pots may be placed in the planter box. In this way, plants that have flowered may retire gracefully to leave space for a fresh pot. Pots placed directly on a window ledge should be placed in a saucer to prevent the wood rotting. There are also

ABOVE: *Miniature roses such as The Fairy can be grown in larger windowboxes such as this, here softened by the tiny flowers of* Erigeron karvinskianus.

LEFT: *A winter flowering windowbox has appeal in cool climates where flowers are few and far between. The small dainty white flowers of the fairy primrose (Primula* malacoides) *rise from a mass of lime green rosette foliage.*

simplelightweight plastic and chrome kits that can be attached to window ledges to hold pots.

Bulbs herald the arrival of spring and look wonderful in windowboxes — hyacinths, tulips, daffodils, grape hyacinths, ranunculas and anenomes in all colours. Geraniums are an age-old favourite as are petunias, alyssum, marigolds, violas, wallflowers, primulas, sweet William and verbena. Windows lined with simple daisies can look stunning. Trailing plants include that wonderful star-white *Campanula isophylla* 'Alba' or the prostrate rosemary. A novel idea would be a native windowbox designed to attract birds or perhaps a vegetable patch windowbox! Possibilities are endless, but some suggestions for rigging the changes season to season:

SUMMER COLOUR: petunias, ivy geraniums, miniature roses, campanulas and daisies.

AUTUMN COLOUR: autumn crocus (*Zephyranthes candida*), Easter daisies.

WINTER COLOUR: fairy primrose (*Primula malacoides*), winter roses (hellebores).

SPRING COLOUR: poppies, polyanthus, tulips, daffodils, scilla, ranunculas and anenomes.

YEAR-ROUND INTEREST: herbs, ferns, natives.

Potted plants dry out quickly and should be monitored closely. They need much tender loving care as well as a good regular dose of fertiliser and occasional soil replenishment. Plants should be repotted when necessary.

ABOVE: *An evergreen windowbox planted with mondo grass is an elegant outdoor window furnishing.*

TOP RIGHT: *The bold foliage and unusual flowers of* Hosta *have been used to great effect in this windowbox, placed under a window rather than on a windowsill.*

RIGHT: *Thyme, rosemary and a button squash grow with little attention in this windowbox.*

OPPOSITE: *Babies tears (Erigeron* karvinskianus) *have self-seeded amongst chives growing in this window box.*

GARDEN STEPS

Steps and stairways!
What delightful fancies with
which to ildly play.
What could be more romantic than
a formal garden stairway,
or more intriguing than brief steps
of boulders?

EDNA WALLING, 1896–1973

Changes in level within a garden can very often be the making of a garden, necessitating the use of steps, walls and terraces. Gardens with some element of architecture, be it formal or natural in appearance, lend an air of permanency and charm, growing more beautiful over the years.

A garden that can be seen at one glance holds no mystery and has little to recommend it. However, add a few steps, hedges or walls to separate areas of the garden, a path or two, and sensitive planting pulled together by a thoughtful design to give the essence of an inspiring garden.

ABOVE: *Curved steps impart an air of elegance to the garden and provide a sense of mystery in the garden beyond. Sea Foam roses, with their delicate shell pink flowers in abundance throughout the warmer months, have been used to soften the stonework.*

LEFT: *Changes in level create interest within the garden and lend an air of permanency. Winding steps such as these hold a certain charm, as their destination is concealed, creating a sense of anticipation.*

LEFT: *In this garden the elegance of curved steps is heightened by the spherical finials atop the brick pedestals. The placing of the steps has been given some thought as the sundial in the middle distance is framed by the pedestals.*

Steps are a strong design element in themselves, often linking the house to the garden, or one level to another. Wide generous steps give a feeling of breadth to the garden and can be made more attractive by the use of landings if a whole flight is to be negotiated. Curved steps impart an air of elegance to the garden while more intimate narrow steps are more suited to the informal garden. A change in direction mid-flight can create interest, revealing different views of the garden.

While steps may be softened by planting, it is important not to let the foliage take over, making negotiation of the steps a preoccupation. As there is a certain rhythm to climbing stairs, it can be disconcerting to have the tread disproportionately wide compared to the rise. The size of steps is an important factor — if the rise is too high, they take greater effort to climb, while

if the tread is too narrow, they can be dangerous without ample room to place the foot. The 'rise' is the vertical height of the steps and should be between 115 mm–190 mm (4 in–7 in) while the 'going', which is the area trodden on, should be no less than 250 mm to a maximum of 395 mm (10 in – 15 1/2 in). A suitable average step for most uses has a 15 cm (6 in) rise and a 38 cm (15 in) tread. Width is also important, and here a comfortable width is 1 m (3 ft) with entry steps wider to allow two people to walk side by side — at least 1.5 m (5 ft).

As with all manner of architecture in the garden, the material should blend with the main theme, be it stone, timber, brick or concrete. Grass verges are an alternative if the slope is gentle, but any slope greater than 25 to 30 per cent makes walking and mowing difficult and is best handled with steps and a retaining wall.

ABOVE: *These old stone steps have been capped with cement to make negotiation smooth. As there is a certain rhythym to climbing stairs, it can be disconcerting to have too uneven a surface, too much foliage covering the steps or disproportionate dimensions.*

RIGHT: *Pockets of flowering ground cover plants have naturalised along the perimeter of these steps, softening the outline and adding interest. Babies' tears (Erigeron karvinskianus), snow-in-summer (Cerastium tomentosum), rose campion (Lychnis coronaria), rock roses (Cistus) and iris flank the path in this rambling country garden.*

BELOW RIGHT: *The charm of this informal flight of steps lies in the understated planting, the soft carpet of fallen spring blossom and the generous width. There is a sense of intimacy in the way the tritelia bulbs and forget-me-nots have naturalised along the perimeter of the steps.*

BARBECUE AREAS

Ohne of the great pleasures in having a garden is escaping from the confines of the house — particularly at meal times. Barbecues provide a marvellously informal way of cooking, eating and entertaining. On a balmy summer's evening, the garden can provide a far more pleasant environment than a hot kitchen.

Such is the popularity of outdoor dining that incorporating a barbecue area can be an important element in your overall garden design and layout. Where space is at a premium, neat unobtrusive gas or electric powered portable barbecues in all shapes and sizes can be placed out of sight after use.

Built-in barbecues need not be unsightly or obtrusive and can be incorporated into a paved seating area with dappled shade from a pergola or mature trees. Stone, brick, concrete block or metal can be used in a multitude of designs. To blend the barbecue in with the surrounding area, it is wise to choose the same material as the paving, walls, steps or home. Perhaps the area can be semi-enclosed by a hedge or plant-covered trellis. Pots of herbs can also draw the eye away from the structure, while adding spice to the cooking.

A B O V E : *An old slow-combustion stove has been converted into an outdoor barbecue in this country garden.*

L E F T : *Built-in barbecues need not be unsightly or obtrusive as this garden shows. Glimpsed through a rose-covered arch and surrounded by old-fashioned perennials and herbs, there is surely enough inducement for outdoor cooking in this garden.*

A generous grill over a firebox is really all that is needed, although more elaborate constructions incorporating wood-box, serving bench, shelves, cupboards and chimney can be useful if space permits. Dimensions are as varied as the designs, but as a general rule, the height of the cooking grate is best situated about 60 cm (2 ft) lower than a standard stove to allow for the long-handled barbeque utensils.

Siting is of utmost importance. Much of the pleasure evaporates if the cook is banished to the far end of the garden and the food cannot be enjoyed 'hot off the barbie'. Easy accessibility to the kitchen is also important so that food and utensils can be carried in and out. There is also more incentive for outdoor meals if an all-weather table and chairs or benches are ready for use rather than having to be put up and put away each time.

A large basket with throwover tablecloth, table napkins, long-handled cooking utensils, large salt and pepper shakers, sauces, mustards, barbecue plates and cutlery can be kept packed in the laundry or pantry for impromptu meals.

ABOVE: *A dry stone wall surrounds this slow-combustion stove barbecue.*

RIGHT: *A formal stone barbecue sited on the banks of a large country lake.*

NEGLECTED CORNERS

*A garden should, I always feel, be just a little
too big to keep the whole cultivated, then it
has a chance to go a little wild in spots, and
make some pictures for you.*

EDNA WALLING, 1896–1973
A Gardener's Log

When the garden stops, fairyland begins' is a saying
that rings in my mind. The hand of nature is
often far more subtle and artistic than our ordered minds
allow and it is true that some of the most enchanting
garden scenes may be found in out of the way corners.
Neglected in a sense, but treasured in another, their very
waywardness in escaping tyranny and order give them a
special quaintness.

These neglected corners often display the most
beautiful plant groupings, with only mother nature to lend
a helping hand. Walking upon such a garden scene is like
finding an attic room that has been locked up for years or
a trunk of old dressing-up clothes — the joy in discovery is
immense.

ABOVE: *The glimpse of a seat tucked away in the corner of a herb garden has a
whimsical air when viewed through a haze of dill.*

LEFT: *Dilapidated pieces of farm machinery, such as this old sub-cover seed
harvester, add rustic appeal to a corner of a garden. The incidental naturalising of
borage, foxgloves and marigolds around the base, only increases the visual appeal.*

ABOVE: *Some of the most enchanting garden scenes are found in out of the way corners.*

LEFT: *A manicured garden is not always the most beautiful to be in. The feeling of wildness and enchantment in unmown areas such as this has an intangible appeal of its own.*

OPPOSITE: *An innovative shed crafted from an overturned tank has been smothered in an Albertine rose.*

As a photographer, I love to wander into the corners of the garden — those areas that, because they are out of general sight, escape the weekly tidy up of the garden proper. In my way of thinking, such areas are the making of many gardens, and are remembered long after the exotic plantings or specimen trees. Even a wheelbarrow, overflowing with weeds and leaves, hastily pushed out of sight and mind behind a hedge has a charm of its own.

There is no blueprint for creating such areas except perhaps to stay well clear and let nature take its course. Unfortunately this is not always a formula for success — most areas left totally untended become completely over-run with weeds rather than romantic havens for foxgloves and forget-me-nots. Of course if you are fortuitous enough to have an old stone ruin

at the bottom of the garden then lend a helping hand by draping it with clematis or wisteria and let nature do the rest.

Gardens that can be viewed at one glance can be disappointing, and even in the smallest area, interest can be heightened by a little concealment. Paths leading around corners, shrubberies concealing hidden corners or lattice used to screen off a service area can all add interest to a garden.

Making garden 'pictures' is half the fun of gardening. Not just growing prime horticultural specimens, but using artistry in creating special areas. Quoting Edna Walling once again: 'So much of that which goes to make up the pictures in gardens has just happened, and so we begin to understand why the gardens of those who are very scientific about them are not always restful

and refreshing. Nothing but that which has been studiously planted by the gardener is allowed to survive. Any natural picture is crushed at the outset, nipped in the bud, cut off at birth!'

Many plants lead a nomadic existence, wandering throughout the garden, self-seeding in unlikely spots, creating their own garden 'pictures'. Foxgloves, poppies, *Erigeron*, larkspurs, love-in-a-mist, honesty and columbines are prolific self-seeders. As many of these plants can swamp the flower garden, seed-heads can be cut off and thrown into the wilder corners of the garden and left to battle for themselves.

Neglected corners are just the site to grow those plants banned from the garden beds — ivies, periwinkles, violets and buttercups. Left to their own devices in out of the way corners, there is little need to be constantly cutting back. It has

been said that a weed is any plant out of place. Rather a harsh judgment, but a judgment often followed by the less romantic gardener who believes that everything has its rightful place. No wayward corners are allowed in their meticulously planned gardens.

Neglected corners do not always magically 'appear'. Much can be said for lending a helping hand. Clothing any unsightly garden structure such as a garden or tool shed, old tree trunk or unsightly fence with a tapestry of scented ramblers (the star jasmine, *Trachelospermum jasminoides*; Chinese wisteria, *Wisteria sinensis*; evergreen clematis, *Clematis armandii*; or evergreen Japanese honeysuckle, *Lonicera japonica*) and underplanting with a carpet of periwinkles, thymes, or violets will soon create a marvellous picture on its own.

BEHIND *the* SCENES:

THE GARDEN SHED AND VINTAGE COMPOST

For where the old thick laurels grow,
along the thin red wall
You find the tool and potting-sheds
which are the heart of all;
The cold frames and the hot houses, the
dungpits and the tanks,
The rollers, carts and drainpipes, with
the barrows and the planks.'

RUDYARD KIPLING, 1865–1936
' The Glory of the Garden'

Just as the contents of the pantry determine the culinary output, the preparation behind the scenes of the garden proper can greatly determine the success of the garden. Given a good potting shed, a couple of compost bins, a wheelbarrow, hose and good garden implements, the keen gardener has the means to create a

---

ABOVE : *An old wattle and daub garden shed provides a backdrop for this collection of garden implements.*

LEFT : *An old sulky and the ladder propped against the shed, presumably leading to an abandoned hayloft, lends a rural charm to this town garden.*

ABOVE LEFT: *The beauty of the potting shed — rustic terracotta pots stacked in readiness.*

LEFT: *Rustic garden implements add much to the atmosphere of this garden shed. A home-made twig broom is kept at hand to brush away cobwebs and sweep the dirt floor of the shed.*

RIGHT: *There is something immensely pleasing in seeing ducks enjoying a stream such as this. Not only do they provide eggs for the pantry, but they have an insatiable appetite for pesky snails.*

horticultural masterpiece. Add a little design knowledge, experience and plant know-how and there is no limit to the possibilities.

This working part of the garden is usually kept behind the scenes and yet it has a fascination all of its own. For aesthetic reasons, the garden shed, compost bins, cold frames and propagation pots are usually hidden at the far corner of the garden but don't be deterred from developing this part of the garden or exploring other people's. I have a quirky fascination with the working area and find it enlightening to see novel methods of propagation in use or perhaps inventive types of compost bins.

There is much to be said in praise of the humble garden shed. Just as Ratty, in *The Wind in the Willows*, loved nothing more than simply messing about in boats, so do many gardeners love messing about in the potting shed, arm deep in potting mix. Edna Walling described the potting shed as 'the most insidious, the most time-

absorbing, the most bewitching spot on the property'.

My ideal garden shed would be an old building (not too small or dark) complete with generous workbench (topped with a window where the light streams in), plenty of shelves (piled with old terracotta pots, jars of seeds, string, catalogues and notebook), bins (filled with fertilisers, lime, potting mixes, sand, blood and bone and peat moss), compost bins close at hand and an old cane chair under the shade of the verandah. At the back door, a large shade cloth structure shelters all the propagated cuttings with water close to hand. In reality, garden sheds are not usually a gardener's retreat, but, however simple, ugly or brand new the building, camouflage is the key. A simple piece of lattice and a year's growth of an evergreen climber, such as the Japanese honeysuckle (*Lonicera japonica*) can do wonders for a shed's appearance and insulation.

LEFT: *An antiquated vegetable cart is still a much used piece of garden equipment in this large kitchen garden. A collection of old sheds provide ample space for the all the equipment needed for gardening, particularly when propagating and growing vegetables.*

OPPOSITE: *Some of the most picturesque garden scenes are actually past the garden fence into the paddocks beyond. The pastoral simplicity of this scene has subtle beauty with chooks nesting and scratching around under the giant eucalypt and rows of fruit trees growing in the background.*

Garden tools are a necessary ingredient and a wise investment. A good strong fork (I have broken two not-so-good, but brand new ones in the past few months), shovel, spade, trowel, hoe, rake, sharp secateurs, saw, watering can and wheelbarrow, if looked after, may last a lifetime. Rubbing the handles with linseed oil occasionally, and religiously storing them out of the weather prolongs their life infinitely.

A simple welded iron or timber structure topped with shadecloth is an ideal place for starting cuttings and raising seeds. Propagation is immensely satisfying and a simple way to develop a garden economically or to perpetuate uncommon, hard to find treasures. No elaborate equipment or knowledge is required, simply a pair of secateurs, clean pots and potting mix (mixture of sand and peat moss or compost). Cuttings may be dipped in a hormone powder to hasten the formation of roots and are usually taken from tip growth or vigorous side shoots. Strip the leaves from the lower half of the cutting

and make a hole in the soil before burying the end in and watering well. Cuttings should be about 10 cm (4 in) long and a number can be put in each pot. Pots should be kept in a sheltered, warm position and kept damp. Cuttings will take two to six weeks to strike. Fortuitously, many of the commendable hedging plants such as box, lavender, santolina, rosemary, *Lonicera nitida* and varieties of rose are simple to strike.

The scientific approach to improving soil and cultivating healthy plants relies considerably on compost, which enriches the soil and puts back all the nutrients taken by the growing plants. Making compost is not greatly dissimilar to putting away a good vintage brew. Certainly much of the vigour and health of the garden depends on the humble compost bin. There is an old gardeners' saying that if it isn't in the soil, it isn't in the plant. By putting in kitchen scraps, weeds, prunings, wood ash, dust from the vacuum cleaner, lawn clippings and manure, seaweed or straw if on hand, a rich fertiliser mulch can be

made, high in nitrogen and carbon. For rapid decomposition, materials should be layered and the heap turned at least once a week. Comfrey is a wonderful compost activator and can be planted against the bin for easy access.

Great ingenuity is displayed in designing compost bins, from the more traditional wooden sleepers to lightweight circular wire mesh bins. Corrugated iron, timber pallets, hay bales, bricks or stone can all be used in many different ways. After years of experimenting with all forms of compost bins, from massive water tanks cut in half to steel post constructions, I have come across the simplest, most easy-on-the-eye construction made in a couple of minutes from old bales of hay. They are simply stacked together to form two large deep bays and no doubt will eventually break down into compost themselves.

Liquid fertilisers using compost, manure or kitchen wastes are also a wonderful source of plant food, releasing many essential elements (nitrogen, potassium and phosphorous) needed by growing plants. Some of the different concoctions include soaking a hessian bag of poultry or stable manure in an old garbage bin filled with water. The same method can be used with soot or a compost tea can be concocted by simply stirring a bucket of compost in a bin of water. A more concentrated form of fertiliser can be made by putting all the kitchen scraps into an open-bottomed plastic bin, adding a spadeful of dirt and handful of dolomite (calcium magnesium carbonate) every now and then and 'curing' for about twelve weeks.

Mulch is the gardener's greatest asset, negating much weeding, digging, watering and fertilising. By covering the soil with a thick layer of readily degradable organic material such as compost, hay, straw, lawn clippings or leaves, a blanketing effect is created, eliminating temperature fluctuations and suppressing weed growth. There are also a high proportion of plant nutrients in mulch which are gradually released into the soil.

CHILDREN'S PLAYGROUNDS

Children, generally, are not sophisticated mites. They can gain as much amusement from a box of sand as from some elaborate toy. What they *do* enjoy, is sunshine, fresh air and plenty of space to run off all that pent-up energy. It is often easier to have a special children's play area within the garden than have the whole area under seige.

This does not necessarily require elaborate constructions. An old tree can make a marvellous cubby (for toddlers) or tree house (for more adventurous older children) with just a few pieces of wood, an old ladder and plenty of imagination. As the latter is something most children have in abundance, such simple structures evoke images of pirate fortresses, deserted islands or simply a place to have a teddy bear's picnic.

A sandpit is the most basic 'must' for young children. Wooden sleepers, treated pine logs or rock boulders can be put together in little time and simply filled with fine sand. If there are roaming cats in the neighbourhood, it may be worth covering the sandpit each night for personal hygiene.

Rubber tyre swings are simple to construct and can provide hours of enjoyment in the shade of an old tree. Similarly, a simple and inexpensive hammock slung

---

ABOVE: *An old-fashioned rocking horse, sheltered from the elements on a wide verandah, provides endless delight to generations of young children.*

LEFT: *Jacaranda blossom carpets the ground and provides a colourful sheltered canopy for a simple swing.*

LEFT: *Simply constructed bush timber play equipment has rustic appeal in this Australian native garden and provides hours of entertainment for a growing family of boys.*

OPPOSITE: *Wooden constructions are more aesthetically pleasing within a garden, blending naturally into the surrounds.*

between two trees can provide endless fun for children and a peaceful retreat for parents as well. Our children were given hammocks one Christmas, and although I didn't get a look in, they were seldom off them the entire holidays. Slung under an old mulberry tree, there were games of swinging them to the limit, pleadings of 'can we sleep outside tonight?' and hours of

simple fun lying in their hammocks telling stories, joking and reading, interspersed by occasional grubby raids on the mulberry tree.

Climbing frames, rope ladders, rockers, see-saws, slippery dips, fortresses and good old-fashioned cubbies are among the many options when contemplating play equipment. Wooden constructions are more aesthetically pleasing in

the confines of the garden than aluminium and steel and can be far more individual and innovative. The timber poles can later be re-used as the children outgrow their equipment. Boulders to climb on and trees to hide behind also hold a special fascination.

As the children grow and move into cricket, soccer and volleyball, a wide open area of lawn, uncluttered by trees or taps is a great asset. Just having a large enough area to rough-and-tumble on can be fun. Children also enjoy being involved in the garden and can relish the idea of having their own garden — even if the enthusiasm comes in fits and starts. Perhaps a few pots of strawberries for starters, or some gourds and sunflowers for the more adventurous.

OPPOSITE: *This cubby house, seen through a hedge of Penelope roses, has been constructed from old packing cases and has provided years of fantasy and enjoyment for many children.*

RIGHT: *A simple swing is the most used piece of children's equipment and does not necessitate an elaborate construction, as this example illustrates. An attractive lattice rose arbour is the ideal place to hang this detachable rope swing which looks wonderfully appealing in its fragrant surrounds of lavenders, foxgloves and climbing roses.*

A novel idea is to designate a special area for each child and start with a well dug-over area and a packet of seeds. Each child can then spell their name on the soil with the seeds. After a few weeks of patient watering, they will (hopefully) be rewarded with their own unique signature garden.

Inner city gardens require special consideration. Perhaps that small outside garden shed could be used for a few years as a cubby and a shaded corner used for a few important years as a sandpit to be later transformed into a pond. Wading pools are sometimes the only choice for tiny paved courtyard gardens. Never disregard the fun children can have with a few cardboard boxes, which, when totally dismembered can be thrown away or recycled. An easel that can be stored in the shed or simply a sheet thrown over a table for a cubby can provide some amusement where space is limited.

SWIMMING POOLS

The incorporation of a swimming pool into a garden can be one of the most demanding landscape projects within the garden area. If the garden has been designed as an object of beauty, the addition of a pool must not attract undue attention. Hidden from general view by a hedge, screen or fence, with attractive surrounds, it need not be a focal point. If, however, a pool is very much part of an overall lifestyle, it need not be hidden but can be carefully integrated into the surrounds.

Perhaps the most off-putting feature of the swimming pool is the glaringly aquamarine blue water which is so obvious within the confines of a small garden. A black lined pool can look stunning and cast off marvellous reflections of the surrounding garden. Alternatively, natural or salt water in a buff coloured pool surrounded by attractive stonework and soft planting can be quite a peaceful scene. Here, practicality must be weighed against aesthetics.

Childproof fencing need not be a dull affair. Brush fencing can offset a natural pool or limed timber and lattice may be more appropriate for a more refined look.

A B O V E : *A pool that is at one in its surrounding is an exacting task to accomplish. This pool has been ingeniously designed using fresh spring-fed water, lined with local stone that blends into the garden surrounds.*

L E F T : *The incorporation of a pool into an old-style home and garden such as this is daunting, but the solicitous choice of paving and colour of water creates a subtle harmony between home and pool. Located in an existing courtyard of an old country home, the pool area is literally a sun trap, with the dark paving and water holding the heat.*

A pergola on one side of the pool can relieve much of the starkness and provide welcome shade during the heat of the day. A scattering of chairs under the shade of a tree also adds ambience. A timber storage box-seat to store pool cleaning equipment and accessories can double as handy seating.

The pool surrounds will give much of the character to the pool setting. Tiles, slate, bush rock, timber or paving will ease the pool into its surroundings. A textured finish will be more slip resistant and tiles will be less maintenance than grass. It is now possible to paint the interior of the pool to match the surrounds with colours ranging from slate, riversand brown, fern, emerald or brook green through a range of blues, buffs, white or black.

Above-ground pools can be thoughtfully integrated into the landscape with a little imag-ination. Kidney-shaped pools are preferable to the ubiquitous round or hexagonal above-ground pools. There are now coloured liners and colour co-ordinated edges to give each pool individuality. Raised timber decking surrounding the pool can give the appearance of an inbuilt pool whilst skilful planting will link the deck and the surrounding garden.

It is the planting surrounding the pool that will give the ultimate character by blending the pool into the landscape. The simpler the planting scheme the more effective. Deep green foliage is preferable to bright lime greens or variegateds and repetition in planting is favoured to bits and pieces of everything. The key to the successful inclusion of a natural-looking pool in the landscape is its sense of 'belonging' — blending plants, fencing, water colour and construction medium in with the home and garden.

ABOVE RIGHT:
Erecting a pleasing child proof surround to the pool is the one element that gives ultimate character. Simplicity is the most effective means of blending a pool into the landscape. Deep green foliage and an elegant Lutyens seat complement the cream-painted trellis in this city pool.

RIGHT: *Not many homes are lucky enough to have a natural swimming hole such as this at the foot of their garden. Deep enough to dive into or swing off ropes from overhanging trees into, all the benefits of having a pool are had without any of the inconveniences of cleaning and filtering.*

OPPOSITE: *A wonderfully inviting pool, with squatter's chairs for lounging in, a large umbrella for shade and surrounding greenery which provides privacy and camouflage for an effective child proof barrier.*

FLORAL ARTISTRY

One of gardening's greatest joys is bringing the garden indoors — filling the home with fragrance, colour and beauty from the garden. Vases brimming with flowers, bowls overflowing with sweetly scented potpourri, herbal wreaths, fragrant bath bags, dried flower topiary trees, swags or garlands, or simply baskets of lavender or dried grasses can instantly rejuvenate tired rooms and jaded spirits.

While floral art was once a skill almost bequeathed from generation to generation, there is now a more relaxed informality in floral displays. Massed arrangements have just as much appeal as tricky artistic concoctions. A plain jar of daisies or bowl of herbs on the kitchen table has a simple charm of its own while a silver water jug abrim with single old-fashioned roses is more of a statement. Bountiful baskets of dried flowers are wonderful adornments to fireplaces during the warmer months and these can be as simple or elegant as the room demands. Much of the effect and appeal lies in the container and placement. Here, expense is not the key, rather a discerning eye for unusual and preferably antiquated containers — often having no semblance to a

ABOVE : *There is now a more relaxed informality in floral displays, with overblown roses mixed in with herbs having as much appeal as tricky artistic arrangements.*

LEFT : *This antique pram brimming with flowers, such as Queen Anne's lace, cosmos, hydrangeas, chrysanthemums and buddleias, is irresistible and shows that receptacles made purely for arrangements are not necessarily the ones with the most panache.*

LEFT: *This simple arrangement of albertine roses shows that in flower arranging great beauty exists in the supreme simplicity of keeping to one variety.*

BELOW: *An eclectic collection of containers has great appeal. Don't overlook a simple enamel pitcher or silver teapot as a suitable container.*

ABOVE: *These hats have been made from natural fibres found within the garden — plaited red hot poker reeds have been used to style the hat, decorated with dried flowers such as statice, honesty, helichrysum and dried roses.*

RIGHT: *Grapevine prunings are simply twisted into wreaths to provide the base for arrangements such as this one, using the grey-green eucalypt leaves which dry so easily, mossy twigs, cones and gum nuts to great effect.*

vase. Pitchers, garden urns, baskets, china bowls, cut glass or silverware can lend that certain touch of individuality to any arrangement. Delicate wreaths and garlands can be made from fresh or dried flowers and have an old world charm all of their own. Each one is totally unique, reflecting the individual's personality. There is no limit to the possibilities: practical herbal wreaths for the cook, scented cottage garden wreaths for a bedroom or wildflower garlands. Bases can be made from wisteria or grape prunings, straw, wire, willow branches or purchased oasis rings. A simple rosemary heart-shaped wreath can be made from an old wire coathanger. Ingenuity is very much part of the dried flower arranger's art.

In times gone past, most gardens included a special picking area. Here flowers were grown purely for picking and could include many

ABOVE: *The pursuit of fragrance has been the essence of the art of potpourri, an ancient pursuit that is surprisingly simple. Traditionally based on the fragrance of scented roses such as these, much of the pleasure in making potpourri is in experimenting with colours, textures and fragrances.*

LEFT: *An old china pitcher brimming with lilies, hemlock, daisies and roses.*

bright colours which would look out of place within the total garden scheme. The 'picking garden' is still very much part of many larger gardens that can afford the room, and a number of friends that dabble in dried flower arrangements have special picking gardens for this purpose. For dried flower purposes, it is not always the flower that is sought after — both the poppy and nigella have seed-heads which look wonderful in dried arrangements, as do onion and garlic heads.

Much of the pleasure of pursuing these activities is in the harvesting. To stroll among the flowers with secateurs in hand and basket in the other, not with the intent of dead-heading or weeding, but for the pure pleasure of collecting the spoils with an eye to a certain arrangement, can be an immensely pleasurable pursuit. While I sometimes feel a certain irreverance in picking the last roses of summer or the first spring bulbs, this is tempered by the fragrance and beauty that fills the room where they are placed.

Fragrance is an ephemeral pleasure — the subtle hint of scent from a vase of flowers is enough to lure you to wander closer to find the source of the fragrance.   This pursuit of fragrance has been the essence of the art of potpourri, an ancient art, older even than the pharaohs. With a tradition so steeped in history, it is thought by many to be a learned craft. It is,

RIGHT: *A garden is the source of many floral crafts including wreaths, dried flower arrangements, baskets and pressed flower compositions. There is total individuality in creating arrangements such as these — each one with a unique charm all of its own.*

however, suprisingly simple and once you develop an eye for colour and fragrance, a whole new dimension is added to gardening. What could be more charming than a bowl of rich carmine rose buds or a blue and white china bowl filled to overflowing with blue delphiniums, larkspurs, lavenders, cornflowers, cloves, cinnamon sticks and white rose petals. A simple dry potpourri is as easy as mixing a handful of dried lavender flowers and dried rose petals, a pinch of orrisroot (fixative) and a drop or two of essential oil in any choice of fragrance. There are of course far more enticing and varied potpourri recipes than this and many books from which to choose them, but here again, experimenting is half the joy.

While not everyone is fortunate to have a still-room, it is suprising where you can find room to hang flowers to dry or scatter petals for potpourri. Dark cupboards are not necessarily needed — just a cool area with good circulation, low moisture and which is preferably out of direct sunlight. Beams in the kitchen, garage or attic; towel racks; bed-ends or old hat racks can be hung with all manner of flowers and foliage while rose petals can be spread on newspaper under a bed or in a spare bedroom. As the harvest is a colourful fragrant one, the bounty can be enjoyed while drying and there is a certain charm in having bunches of paeonies, gypsophila or delphiniums hang-drying from the beams.

FINISHING TOUCHES

Garden accessories go a long way towards accomplishing the final garden picture and evoking a feeling of ambience. Finishing touches such as garden lighting, name plates, letter boxes, finials, pedestals, wall plaques, plinths, taps, umbrellas and weather vanes bring life to the garden framework.

These personal touches bring out the character of the person behind the garden and reflect their individual style and originality. Bits and pieces from travels and friends add interest and personalise a garden. As in interior design or fashion, it is the accessories that determine the outcome.

Lighting is often one of the most effective way of highlighting features in the garden — a tree trunk or canopy, a piece of sculpture, an outdoor living area or entrance gates and doors. In most cases, lighting considerations are left till last, necessitating complicated and expensive installation. It should be considered in the original garden design if starting from scratch. Free standing wrought iron street lamps are an elegant feature while wall brackets can be chosen in a host of styles.

ABOVE : *Individually hand-painted name plates add whimsy to a garden setting. This little guest cottage had long been named 'Toad Hall' so it was with great delight that this plaque was found.*

LEFT : *Personal touches individualise a garden, bringing out the character of the person behind the garden and reflecting an individual style and originality. A rustic wreath fashioned from grapevine and pomegranate fruit adds character to this back entrance with an old wool basket and antiquated wheelbarrow providing attractive receptacles for storing wood and kindling.*

L E F T :   *These attractive*
wall lamps lend a touch of
elegance to a front entrance.

O P P O S I T E :   *An old*
well lends atmosphere to this
miner's cottage garden.

Bird houses or dovecotes can be perched on stilts or hung from a tree to en-courage birds into the garden. More than shelter or food, water is the essential clement in attracting birds into a garden. Even on the coldest winter mornings, they love to bathe and play in the water. If there are no cats in the vicinity, large shallow dishes can be left under dripping taps (birds love fresh water) or simple rough hewn bird baths can be made from sand-coloured conrete and can be surrounded by moss-covered or lichen-crusted boulders. Where there are cats in the garden, bird baths should be erected on pedestals at least 1.5 m (5 ft) high.

On a larger scale, gazebos or summer houses add a wonderfully romantic feeling to a garden, providing a restful shaded retreat. Furnished with comfortable wicker or twig chairs heaped with cushions and a small table large enough to put trays for afternoon tea or lunch,

ABOVE LEFT: *Late afternoon sun bathes this weathered Anduze pot in warm sunlight, a perfect foil against the rich terracotta-coloured wall. A touch of greenery is provided by the simple white geranium in the pot and the white violet at the base of the elegant water trough.*

LEFT: *This magnificent aviary is a charming example of garden architecture from last century. It is the oldest surviving aviary in the Australian state of Victoria, and has long been home to many finches and canaries.*

ABOVE RIGHT:
*Name plates add
individuality to the simplest
garden entrance.*

RIGHT: *Garden
lighting brings life to the
garden in the evening, but
the style of fittings need to be
in keeping with the garden.*

they evoke images of carefree summer days. To add to the aura, these simple structures can be adorned with scented climbers. Old-fashioned scented roses are one of the most popular choices, but care must be taken to choose thornless varieties such as Kathleen Harrop, a fragrant pink rose, constantly in flower; the almost thornless white climbers Mme Legras de Saint Germain or Summer Snow; the dainty shell pink buttonhole rose, Cécile Brunner or the fragrant pink shrub roses, Henri Foucquier or Duchesse d'Angoulême. The banksia rose is thornless but its profuse growth can be a problem for small structures.

Finally, the colour and texture of window awnings, cushion covers or tablecloths add visual interest and visually extend the interior of the home into the garden. Individual hand-picked treasures will add a sense of intrigue to the simplest settings.

ACKNOWLEDGEMENTS

During the course of this book I have visited countless gardens seeking photographs and finding inspiration. To the following people I offer my thanks: Sue Fox, Hedge House, Beechworth; Diana Lempriere, Banongil, Skipton; Raymond Williams, Dalvui, Terang; Jennie Mather, Barbara Perry and Penny Smith, Bleak House, Daylesford; Lady Law-Smith, Bolobek, Macedon; Luki Weatherly, Woolongoon, Mortlake; Belinda Winter-Irving and Paul Mason, Glenlyon, Daylesford; Penny Dunn, Dream-thorpe, Mt Macedon; Heide Kitchen Garden, Bulleen; John Gowty, Buda, Castlemaine; Kuringai Cottage, Wangaratta South; Joy and Eric Sartori, Truro, Daylesford; Celia Burnham, Mt Boninyong, Scotsburn; Elizabeth Gilfillan, Eyre Cottage, Buninyong; Bruce Stafford, Brim Brim, Buninyong; Verity and David Scales, Eurambeen, Beaufort; Mr and Mrs Hewitt, Oomoo, Derrin-allum; Heather Sandford and Mrs Campbell, Hillside, Beaufort; Helen Gordon, Beaumauris, Beechworth; Susie Clarke, Devon Park, Dunkeld; Clive and Margaret Winmill, Badger's Keep, Chewton; Jenny Whitehead, Spring Creek, Hawkesdale; Mrs Manifold, Boortkoi, Hexham; Mrs Murray, Langley Vale, Kyneton; Trish and Maurie Bull, Waiwere, Mansfield; the Ryrie family, Micalago Station, Michelago; Marcia Voce, Birchfield Herbs, Bungendore; Mrs Helen Watson, Mt Annan, Holbrook; Diana Wilson and Joan Downes, Brownlow Hill, Camden; the McIntosh family, Denbigh, Cobbity; Michael Love, Darling Point; Di Polkinghorn, Woollahra;

Kate Anderson, Sydney; Ros Espie, Darling Point; Genevieve Cummins, Pymble; Mary-Louise and Andrew Churchill, Lindfield; Michael Cooke, Belrose Nursery; The Parterre Garden, Woollahra; Robin Jeffcoat, Longfield, Robertson; Rob Tooth, Bungarabee, Marulan; Riversdale, Goulburn; Joan Arnold, Buskers End, Mittagong; Cynthia Parker, Frensham, Mittagong; Mrs Diana Burns, Moidart, Bowral; Mr and Mrs Neil Cottee, Patchways, Burradoo; Dr and Mrs Webber, Toorale, Bowral; Lori Lollbach, Cooma; Mr and Mrs Berzins, Cooma; Pam Glasson, Llangrove, Cooma; Joy Cottle, Shirley, Nimmitabel; Betty Casey-Litchfield, Coolringdon, Cooma; Bett Haslingden, Kelton Plain, Cooma; Barb Litchfield, Hazeldean, Cooma; Annie Kater, Red Cliff, Bombala; Noni Larritt, Woodstock, Cooma; Libby and Jim Litchfield, Myalla, Cooma; Fiona and Joan Massy, Severn Park, Cooma; Marg Herbert, Mia Mia, Nimmitabel; Mrs Betty Osborne, Maffra, Cooma; Stephanie and Patrick Litchfield, Springwell, Cooma; Susie Jardine, Curry Flat, Nimmitabel; Joey Herbert, Nandawar, Kybean; Kathy Jeffreys, Delegate Station, Delegate; Judy Pfeiffer, Cloyne, Cooma; Diana Klima, Cooma; Gay Epstein, Travellers Rest, Cooma; Hilda Wallace, Cooma; Jo and Rowan Dixon, Sentry Box, Yaouk; Susie Lapin, Sydney; Jackie Armes, Trapalanda, Murrumbateman; Sylvia McCoy, Carwoola, Bungendore; Wesley Hamblion and Peter White, the Parsonage, Bungonia; Geoff and Rhondda Cleary, Pialligo Plant Farm, Canberra; Polly Park, Boxford, Red

OPPOSITE: *The essence of the garden lies in that fragile equilibrium between imposing our own will and letting nature take its course. In this wild garden, nature lies undisturbed — constantly changing yet quixotic in its natural beauty.*

Hill, Canberra; Rodney's Nursery, Pialligo, Canberra; Gavin Doherty and Tina Fraser, Out of Town Nursery, Beechworth; Rose Cottage, Beechworth; the Jory and the Bunting families from Beechworth; Sweet Violets, Mosman; Carmel Wagstaff, Brunette Downs, Northern Territory; Mary Emmott, Noonbah, Stonehenge, Queensland; and certainly not least, my parents, Neville and Margaret Burkitt, Spring Ponds, Bungonia.

Also for correspondence and assistance from Mrs Pat Weatherly, Mortlake; Heather Chadwick, Sydney; Linley Vellacott, Melbourne; Mrs Karen Mackinnon, Mt Macedon; Mrs Elizabeth Rowe, Naringal; Mrs Pat Kater, Scone; Elizabeth Symonds and Keva North from Bowral; Pen Hoskins, Moss Vale; Rowena Weir, Bowning; Dan Ridley, Beechworth. I would also like to thank the staff at the Weston School of Horticulture, in particular, Shirley Brittain for her thought provoking landscape design lectures and the library for their wide selection of reference material. The Cooma library has also been totally denuded of their entire gardening section during the course of this book. Caroline at Chenka Bookshop in Canberra has been helpful tracking down obscure titles and the National Library, Canberra has been a constant back-up.

All attempts have been made to obtain copyright clearance from published works, and I would like to thank the following individuals and publishers: Barbara Baines from Queensland, Australia; Stephen Lacey, UK; McMillan Publishers, New York; and the Literary Trustees of Walter de la Mare and the Society of Authors as their representative.

On the photography side, assistance from Kodak has been invaluable, with particular thanks to Mark Lee. Taking the photos and putting them together in a cohesive form is the essence of the book and my thanks to the Publishers, particularly Kim Anderson for her encouragement and expertise; Ruth Sheard for her kind editing and Kathryn Evans as assistant editor; Liz Seymour and Linda Maxwell for their preliminary photographic selection; and Karen Carter for her patience and expertise in handling the design and layout.

My husband, Darvall, has suffered culinary neglect and horticultural excess throughout the book but has stoically offered encouragement and support and kept the garden going in my absences. Our children, Skye and Hamish, have shared their existence with tripods, cameras, computer and gardens but have remained full of enthusiasm for the project. My wonderful parents, whose garden and boundless energy never cease to be an inspiration to me, have given constant support.

PHOTOGRAPHIC NOTES

Photographs are paramount in a book on garden styles. Just as an artist needs the stimulation of looking at other artists' works, so do gardeners need to visually assess other gardens as well as delve into books on plants and design. A carefully selected picture can convey a message far more eloquent than words and for this reason I make no apologies for the visual emphasis in this book. So often a solution to an area of a garden may be solved through visiting a garden or studying a photograph in a book or magazine.

However, it must be remembered that photographs only portray a transitory image in a garden. It may be that some gardens are superb for only one month of the year, and this is the time, of course, when gardeners want the photographer to visit. When studying garden photographs, it is worth looking beyond the artistic composition and trying to establish what would hold a particular garden together in another season. Study the plant combinations, colours and design layout. As a photographer, I am constantly looking for lines of axis, vistas and strong design elements. Simple gardens of trees and ground covers may well be some of the most restful to be in, but they do not photograph well and for this reason, most photographs have some architectural or design element.

The amount of light in the garden goes a long way to adding atmosphere and anyone who wanders in their garden as the sun rises or who gardens well into dusk can enjoy the soft filtered light, so different to the harsh midday sun. This has meant the constant use of tripods to allow the slower shutter speeds necessary for the reduced light and depth of field. A low ASA film was chosen for quality of reproduction in enlargement. For premium picture quality, I used Kodachrome professional 64 ASA color reversal film. My thanks go to Mark Lee at Kodak (Australasia) Pty Ltd for their generosity and to the Schoo Family at Schoo's Photographic Studio in Cooma. Three cameras were used — a twin lens Rolleicord, and two 35 mm Nikons.

My trusty ancient Rolleicord camera is perhaps my most treasured possession. Purchased second-hand years ago for a mere song, this wonderful piece of pre-Word War II equipment has none of the modern aids such as light meter, automatic focus, zoom lens or motor drive. It *does* have a superb precision ground lens, a waist-level view finder perfect for photo composition and it is without batteries or gadgetry which have a knack of going awry in the most far-flung locations. Perched on a sturdy tripod, it is the perfect tool for surveying the garden. Certainly it heightens ones appreciation of a garden as the images all look so wonderful through the camera lens. The fact that this camera is the choice of many 'thinking' photographers, including Edna Walling, whose photography has an ageless evocativeness, reinforces my faith in this wonderful piece of equipment.

PHOTOGRAPHIC LOCATIONS

Front cover: Kelton Plain, Cooma, NSW.
Back cover: Micalago Station, Michelago, NSW.
Prelims: i Rustic rose arbour — Buda, Castlemaine, Victoria; iv Steps — Springwell, Cooma, NSW; v Pergola covered terrace — Hazeldean, Cooma, NSW; vi Pergola — Sturt, Mittagong, NSW; vii Geese — Springwell, Cooma, NSW.
Garden Styles: x-1 Rose cottage — Beechworth, Victoria. Photo: Lorna Rose.
The Classical Garden: 2 Tulips and forget-me-nots — Moidart, Bowral, NSW; 3 *Lilium candidum* — Bobundara, Cooma, NSW; 4 Spring vista — Bolobek, Macedon, Victoria; 5 Dovecote — Bolobek, Macedon, Victoria; Urn — Dalvui, Terang, Victoria; 6 Urn — Bolobek, Macedon, Victoria; 7 Daffodils — Bolobek, Macedon, Victoria.
The Cottage Garden: 8 Larkspurs — Brownlow Hill, Camden, NSW; 9 Single opium poppy — Bobundara, Cooma, NSW; 10 Spring blossom — Hillside, Beaufort, Victoria; 11 Cottage garden — Cathcart Street, Goulburn, NSW; 12 Cottage path — Birchfield, Bungendore, NSW; 13 Spring poppies — Toorale, Bowral, NSW; 14 Miner's cottage garden — Beaumauris, Beechworth, Victoria; Cottage garden — Badger's Keep, Chewton, Victoria; 15 Historic cottage garden — Denbigh, Cobbitty, NSW; 16 Picket fence — Buckland Gallery, Beechworth, Victoria; 17 Sheep in orchard — Hillside, Beaufort, Victoria.
The Romantic Garden: 18 Rustic bridge — Toorale, Bowral, NSW; 19 *Aquilegia vulgaris* — Bobundara, Cooma, NSW; 20 Statue — Coolringdon, Cooma, NSW; Sundial in snow — Bobundara, Cooma, NSW; 21 Bridge — Coolringdon, Cooma, NSW; 22 Lilies in lake — Longfield, Robertson, NSW; 23 Erigeron — Yandra, Nimmitabel, NSW, Garden of Peter and Mary Haylock.
The Country Garden: 24 Bluestone homestead — Devon Park, Dunkeld, Victoria; 25 Sunflower — Traveller's Rest, Cooma, NSW; 26 Rural charm — Kelton Plain, Cooma, NSW; 27 Farmyard — Traveller's Rest, Cooma, NSW; 28 Elm Driveway — Coolringdon, Cooma, NSW; Rustic aviary — Brownlow Hill, Camden, NSW; Bushland setting — Sentry Box, Yaouk, NSW; 29 Verandah — Espie Home, Darling Point, NSW; 30 Pastoral charm — Brownlow Hill, Camden, NSW; 31 Oak Tree — Delegate Station, Delegate, NSW.
The Fragrant Garden: 32 Scented profusion — Bungarabee, Marulan, NSW; 33 The Reeve — Hedge House, Beechworth, Victoria; 34 Sunken rose garden — Polkinghorn garden, Woollahra, NSW; Wisteria on pergola — Boortkoi, Hexham, Victoria; 35 Bird's eye view — Hedge House, Beechworth, Victoria; 36 Wisteria — Busker's End, Bowral, NSW; 37 Spring ranunculas — Patchway, Burradoo, NSW.
The Wild Garden: 38 Fairy tale walk — Coolringdon, Cooma, NSW; 39 Teasel — Birchfield, Bungendore, NSW; 40 Haze of blue — Devon Park, Dunkeld, Victoria; 41 Bare trunks — Bobundara, Cooma, NSW; Spring bulbs — Langley Vale, Kyneton, Victoria; 42 Ethereal driveway — Myalla, Cooma, NSW; 43 Gate ajar — Coolringdon, Cooma, NSW; 44 Early spring — Shirley, Nimmitabel, NSW; 45 Boat moored in lake — Dreamthorpe, Macedon, Victoria.
The Herb Garden: 46 Bathtub of herbs — Birchfield Herbs, Bungendore, NSW; 47 White borage — Bobundara, Cooma, NSW; 48 Sundial — Banongil, Skipton, Victoria; 49 Rustic herb garden — Eyre Cottage, Buninyong, Victoria; Watering can — Birchfield, Bungendore, NSW; 50 Garden rake — Birchfield,

Bungendore, NSW; 51 Herb vinegars — Bobundara, Cooma.
The Rose Garden: 52 Summer house — Birchfield, Bungendore, NSW; 53 Wedding Day rose — Birchfield, Bungendore, NSW; 54 Sunken rose garden — Mt Annan, Holbrook, NSW; 55 Gloire Lyonnaise — Bobundara, Cooma, NSW; Single rugosa rose — Patchway, Burradoo, NSW; 56 Constance Spry rose — Bobundara, Cooma, NSW; Thyme and rose — Beaumauris, Beechworth, Victoria; 57 Rose swag — Busker's End, Bowral, NSW.
The Courtyard Garden: 58 Courtyard — Kelton Plain, Cooma, NSW; 59 Harbour courtyard — Michael Love, Darling Point, NSW; 60 Historic courtyard — Denbigh, Cobbitty, NSW; 61 Elegant setting — Michael Love, Darling Point, NSW; Courtyard pond — Kelton Plain, Cooma, NSW; 62 Inner courtyard — Kelton Plain, Cooma, NSW; 63 Formal courtyard — Michael Love, Darling Point, NSW.
The Kitchen Garden: 64 Kitchen garden — Rose Cottage, Beechworth, Victoria; 65 Pears — Klima garden, Cooma, NSW; 66 Kitchen plot — Eurambeen, Beaufort, Victoria; Watering cans — Traveller's Rest, Cooma, NSW; 67 Late afternoon — Truro, Daylesford, Victoria; 68 Scarecrow — by Skye Dixon, Bobundara, Cooma, NSW; 69 No-dig kitchen garden — Waiwere, Mansfield, Victoria.
The Naturalist's Garden: 70 Sea of daffodils — Banongil, Skipton, Victoria; 71 Spider web — Bobundara, Cooma, NSW; 72 Reflections — Banongil, Skipton, Victoria; Snow scene — Bobundara, Cooma, NSW; 73 Shaded pathway — Moidart, Bowral, NSW.
Old-fashioned Gardens: 74 Old-fashioned garden — Riversdale, Goulburn, NSW; 75 Love-in-a-mist — Bobundara, Cooma, NSW; 76 Box edging — Mt Boninyong, Victoria; 77 Rural charm — Spring Ponds, Bungonia, NSW; 78 Sundial — The Parsonage, Bungonia, NSW; Driveway — Denbigh, Cobbitty, NSW; 79 Late afternoon and lily — The Parsonage, Bungonia, NSW.
Garden Seasons: 80-81 Lawn daisies — Dreamthorpe, Macedon, Victoria.
The Spring Garden: 82 Sundial — Eurambeen, Beaufort, Victoria; 83 Oriental poppy — Birchfield, Bungendore, NSW; 84 Country driveway — Langley Vale, Kyneton, Victoria; *Tulipa saxatilis* — Eurambeen, Beaufort, Victoria; 85 Sunken garden — Moidart, Bowral, NSW; 86 Stone wall — Banongil, Skipton, Victoria; 87 Courtyard garden — Hedge House, Beechworth, Victoria.
The Garden in Summer: 88 Shady verandah — Espie home, Darling Point, NSW; 89 Canterbury bells — Birchfield, Bungendore, NSW; 90 Lavender walk — Wilson garden, Brownlow Hill, Camden, NSW; Delphiniums — Bobundara, Cooma, NSW; 91 Country pool — Mt Annan, Holbrook, NSW; 92 White border — Bobundara, Cooma, NSW; 93 Wedding Day rose — Birchfield Herbs, Bungendore, NSW.
The Garden in Autumn: 94 Elms — Coolringdon, Cooma, NSW; 95 Crataegus berries — Bobundara, Cooma, NSW; 96 Driveway — Coolringdon, Cooma, NSW; 97 Autumn leaves — Bobundara, Cooma, NSW; 98 Leafy walk — Coolringdon, Cooma, NSW; 99 Drying herbs — Bobundara, Cooma, NSW; Pergola — Hazeldean, Cooma, NSW.
The Winter Garden: 100 Snowscape — Hazeldean, Cooma, NSW; 101 *Eryngium bourgatii* — Bobundara, Cooma, NSW; 102 Glimpse of homestead — Hazeldean, Cooma, NSW; 103 Silhouette — Bobundara, Cooma, NSW; 104 Stone homestead

BIBLIOGRAPHY

BISGROVE, Richard, *The Flower Garden.* Collins Publishers, Sydney, 1989

BLIGH, Beatrice, *Cherish the Earth.* Ure Smith Sydney, 1973

BROOKES, John, *The Country Garden.* Dorling Kindersley, London, 1987

BROWN, Jane, *Vita's Other World: A Gardening Biography of Vita Sackville-West.* Penguin, England, 1987

BROWN, Jane, *Gardens of a Golden Afternoon.* Penguin, England, 1987

CUFFLEY, Peter, *Cottage Gardens in Australia.* Five Mile Press, Melbourne, 1983

CUFFLEY, Peter, *Creating Your Own Period Garden.* Five Mile Press, Melbourne, 1984

DEANS, Esther, *Esther Deans' Gardening Book: growing without digging.* Harper and Row, Sydney, 1977

DIXON, Trisha and CHURCHILL, Jennie, *Gardens in Time: In the Footsteps of Edna Walling.* Angus and Robertson, Sydney, 1988

FELTWELL, John, *The Naturalist's Garden.* Edbury Press, London, 1987

GALBRAITH, Jean, *Garden in a Valley.* Five Mile Press, Melbourne, 1985

GALBRAITH, Jean, *A Garden Lover's Journal 1943–1946.* Five Mile Press, Melbourne, 1989

GRIFFITHS, Trevor, *My World of Old Roses.* Whitcoulls Publishers, Christchurch (NZ), 1983

HOBHOUSE, Penelope, *Garden Style.* Georgian House, Melbourne, 1988

HOBHOUSE, Penelope, *The Country Gardener.* Frances Lincoln Ltd, London, 1989

HOBHOUSE, Penelope (ed.), *Gertrude Jekyll on Gardening.* Vintage Books, New York, 1985

JEKYLL, Gertrude, *The Making of a Garden.* Antique Collectors' Club, England, 1984

JEKYLL, Gertrude (with Edward Mawley), *Roses for English Gardens .* Penguin Books, 1983

JOHNSON, Hugh, *The Principles of Gardening.* Mitchell Beazley, London, 1979

KELLY, Frances, *A Simple Pleasure: the art of garden making in Australia.* Methuen, Australia, 1982

LACEY, Stephen, *The Startling Jungle.* Penguin, England, 1987

LAW-SMITH, Joan, *The Uncommon Garden.* The Women's Committee of the National Trust of Australia (Victoria), 1983

LAW-SMITH, Joan, *A Gardener's Diary.* The Women's Committee of the National Trust of Australia (Victoria), 1976

LLOYD, Christopher and BIRD, Richard, *The Cottage Garden.* Dorling Kindersley, London, 1990

MASSINGHAM, Betty, *Miss Jekyll.* David and Charles, London, 1966

McLEOD, Judyth, *Our Heritage of Old Roses.* Kangaroo Press, Sydney, 1987

MURRAY, Elizabeth and FELL, Derek, *Home Landscaping ... Ideas, Styles and Designs for Creative Outdoor Spaces.* Simon and Schuster, New York

NICHOLSON, Nigel, *Portrait of a Marriage.* Weidenfeld& Nicolson, London, 1983

NOTTLE, Trevor, *Growing Old-Fashioned Roses in Australia and New Zealand.* Kangaroo Press, 1983

OSLER, Mirabel, *A Gentle Plea for Chaos.* Bloomsbury, London, 1989

PAGE, Russell, *The Education of a Gardener.* Collins, London, 1962

PAUL, Anthony and REES, Yvonne, *The Garden Design Book.* Collins, London, 1988

PHILLIPS, Roger and RIX, Martyn, *Roses.* Pan Books, London, 1988

PIRIE, Chris, *The Australian Scented Garden.* Harper and Row, Sydney, 1984

PROUDFOOT, Helen, *Gardens in Bloom.* Kangaroo Press, 1989

ROBINSON, William, *The Wild Garden.* Century Hutchison Ltd/The National Trust, London, 1983

ROBINSON, William, *English Flower Garden.* John Murray London, 1883

ROSE, Graham, *The Romantic Garden.* William Collins, Australia 1988

ROSE, Graham, *The Traditional Garden Book.* Greenhouse Publications, Australia, 1989

SAVILLE, Diana, *Gardens for Small Country Houses.* Viking, London, 1988

SCHINZ, Marina, *Visions of Paradise: Themes and Variation on the Garden.* Thames and Hudson, London, 1985

SCOTT-JAMES, Anne, *Sissinghurst: The Making of a Garden.* Michael Joseph Ltd, London, 1975

STEEN, Nancy, *The Charm of Old Roses.* A. H. and A. W. Reed, Auckland, 1966

STONES, Ellis, *Australian Garden Design.* Macmillan, Melbourne, 1971

SQUIRE, David, *The Scented Garden.* Doubleday, Australia, 1989

SUDELL, Richard, *Landscape Gardening.* Ward, Lock and Co. Ltd, London, 1933

TANNER, Howard and BEGG, Jane, *The Great Gardens of Australia.* Macmillan, Melbourne, 1976

THOMAS, Graham Stuart, *The Old Shrub Roses,* Phoenix House Ltd, London, 1955

THOMAS, Graham Stuart, *Shrub Roses of Today.* Phoenix House Ltd, London, 1962

THOMAS, Graham Stuart, *A Garden of Roses.* Pavilion Books Ltd, London, 1987

TOLLEY, Emelie and MEAD, Chris, *Herbs.* Sidgwick and Jackson, London, 1985

VEREY Rosemary, *The Garden in Winter.* Frances Lincoln Ltd, 1988

WALLING, Edna, *Gardens in Australia.* Oxford University Press, Melbourne, 1946

WALLING, Edna, *The Edna Walling Book of Australian Garden Design.* Anne O'Donovan, Melbourne, 1981

WALLING, Edna, *On the Trail of Australian Wildflowers.* Mulini Press, Canberra, 1984

WALLING, Edna, *A Gardener's Log.* Anne O'Donovan, Melbourne, 1985

WALLING, Edna, *Country Roads: The Australian Roadside Pioneer.* Design Studio, 1985

WATTS, Peter, *The Gardens of Edna Walling.* National Trust of Victoria, 1982

WILSON, Glen, *Landscaping with Australian Plants.* Nelson, Melbourne, 1975

WHITE, Katharine, *Onward and Upward in the Garden.* McGraw-Hill Ryerson Ltd, Toronto, 6th ed., 1981

INDEX

(Numbers in *italics* indicate the pages where photographs appear.)